About this book 4

best 49–60

where to ... 61–86

travel facts 87–93

About this book

KEY TO SYMBOLS

✚ map reference on the fold-out
map accompanying this book
(see below)

⊠ address

☎ telephone number

🕒 opening times

🍴 restaurant or café on premises
or nearby

🚆 nearest train station

🚌 nearest bus route

🚢 nearest riverboat or ferry stop

♿ facilities for visitors with
disabilities

✋ admission charge

↔ other nearby places of interest

❓ tours, lectures or special events

➤ indicats the page where you will
find a fuller description

ℹ tourist information

CityPack Dublin is divided into six sections to cover the most important aspects of
your visit to Dublin. It includes:

- An overview of the city and its people
- Itineraries, walks and excursions
- The top 25 sights to visit
- Features about different aspects of the city that make it special
- Detailed listings of restaurants, hotels, shops and nightlife
- Practical information

In addition, text boxes provide fascinating extra facts and snippets, highlights of
places to visit and invaluable practical advice.

CROSS-REFERENCES

To help you make the most of your visit, cross-references, indicated by ➤, show
you where to find additional information about a place or subject.

MAPS

The fold-out map in the wallet at the back of the book is a comprehensive street
plan of Dublin. All map references in this book refer to this map. For example, the
National Gallery on Merrion Square West has the following information ✚ L9
indicating the grid square of the map in which the National Gallery will be found.
The city-centre maps found on the inside front and back of the book itself are for
quick reference. They show the Top 25 Sights, described on pages 24–48, which
are clearly plotted by number (**❶ – ㉕**, not page number) from west to east across
the city.

PRICES

An indication of the admission charge (for all attractions) is given by categorising
the standard adult rate as follows:
Expensive (over IR£7), Moderate (IR£3.50–IR£7) and Inexpensive (under
IR£3.50).

CityPack
Dublin

DR PETER HARBISON
AND MELANIE MORRIS

*Dr Peter Harbison, Honorary
Editor of the Royal Irish
Academy, is a former editor of*
Ireland of the Welcomes
*magazine. He is the author of
numerous books on Irish
archaeology, art and architecture.*
Ancient Ireland *(1996), a book
he co-edited with photographer
Jacqueline O'Brien, has appeared
in English and German. Melanie
Morris is the publisher and editor
of* dSide, *Ireland's leading style
magazine.*

City-centre
map continues
on inside back
cover

AA Publishing

Contents

DUBLIN
life

INTRODUCING DUBLIN

Fine Dublin stucco-work – Diana by Michael Stapleton (1765) in Belvedere House

Lights, camera, action!

Ireland's buoyant film industry has made Dublin a popular location for indigenous and foreign productions, and directors such as Neil Jordan and Jim Sheridan have filmed in and around the capital. Scenes from *My Left Foot, Educating Rita, Far and Away, Michael Collins, The Butcher Boy, Nora* (the film of James Joyce starring Ewan McGregor), *Ordinary Decent Criminal* and the latest Disney movie *The Count of Monte Christo* will become familiar as you explore the city where the locals are more than willing to boast about their 15 minutes of location fame!

Founded by the Vikings more than one thousand years ago, Dublin holds the winning ticket when it comes to location. Mountains, green fields and coastline mark the city limits and the wide open spaces of Phoenix Park breathe life into the centre. The River Liffey cuts through from west to east, shaping the city into two seemingly distinct halves – a densely populated, working class district to the north giving way to a more affluent and privileged area in the south – but look closer and you will find many exceptions and contradictions on both sides of the river.

Dublin was transformed in the 18th century by the vision of its Georgian architects. Subsequent modernisation has largely worked in harmony with their designs and contributed to a new urban landscape. The all-glass frontage of the Financial Services Centre soars above the city's old port on the north side, while Temple Bar, behind the quays on the south bank of the Liffey, is an omnium-gatherum of contemporary architecture, converted warehouses and rediscovered buildings along the cobbled streets between the river and busy Dame Street.

Economic progress has brought about dramatic changes but Dublin retains a human dimension that newcomers find appealing. The pace of life is a half beat slower than in any other bustling capital, and there is always time to pause and enjoy the city. With the growth and location of service, computer and hi-tech industries in Dublin, unemployment is at an all time low and the prosperity has kept the young at home and helped reverse the flow of emigration, bringing many Dubliners back from overseas. Their experience of different cultures, combined with a steady influx of visitors, gives the capital a truly international flavour.

In the past decade, Dublin habits have changed quite dramatically – no more so than with where Dubliners live, when they start work, and how they get there. The number of cars on Irish roads has risen dramatically, which means that work starting times – traditionally relatively late in comparison to their European cousins – are being pushed to earlier in the day to try and beat the gridlock. Furthermore, due to the massive hikes in property prices, Dubliners, who prefer to live in houses than apartments, are now living further out of the city – many commuting from counties as far away as Carlow, Meath, Kildare and Wicklow, adding to the daily traffic chaos.

With the new prosperity, the arts are booming, culture is everywhere and there's a palpable sense that this is a friendly city brimming with youth and vitality, while maintaining tradition. Street vendors line the byways and thorough-fares of the bustling shopping district around Grafton Street, tempting passers-by with flowers and jewellery. You could be entertained by any-thing from a string quarter to a single man play-ing percussion on his knees with two empty Coke bottles! Across the river in Moore Street, sturdy women selling fruit, vegetables, pop posters and chocolate from prams, evoke mod-ern-day images of Molly Malone, the fish-selling heroine of Dublin's rousing anthem. Antique charm pervades the pubs, cafés and bars, con-trasting happily with the more cosmopolitan airs of the many fine restaurants, elegant boutiques and lively clubs.

The name

The origins of the city's name can be traced back to the Viking warriors who landed off Ireland's east coast in the 9th century. They set up a trading post by the river and called it Dyflin, after the Irish *dubh linn* meaning 'black pool'. Four centuries later, the Normans captured the city and latinised the name to Dublinia. The modern Irish name, Baile Átha Cliath, 'the settlement of the ford of the hurdles', commemo-rates an ancient ford across the River Liffey.

Anna Livia – *the River Liffey, looking upstream towards the dome of the Four Courts*

Rush hour

The main arteries in and out of Dublin pulse with activity at rush hour. In the morning, paper girls and boys run up and down the intersections selling the *Irish Times* and the *Independent*, returning with the *Evening Herald* later in the day. Marketing girls frequently join in the action, handing out product samples and coupons to unsuspecting motorists waiting anxiously for the traffic lights to change.

The old-world Long Hall Pub in South Great George's Street attracts light-hearted drinkers and serious talkers

Café culture in Dublin is flourishing. With even a hint of sunshine, patrons spill onto the pavements to enjoy some local atmosphere with their food order. Along the Grand Canal, drinkers from the many pubs often enjoy an extended lunch break by the banks, especially on Fridays when evening rush hour seems to unofficially move from 5PM to 2PM.

Once Saturday nights were sacred to cosmopolitan city slickers, now Thursdays are proving just as popular. Young Dubliners have great stamina, often going out three or four times a week, enjoying clubbing, eating out, or a film. True to its roots, drinking is still a big pastime in Dublin, whether it's a quick pint after work or a pub crawl around the city centre.

Healthier Dubliners are spoilt with parks, squares and fields dotted around the city, the most well known being the Phoenix Park. Dubliners congregate in this huge open space to play rugby or football; to cycle or simply to enjoy a picnic. Other city parks with tennis courts and football pitches are Bushy Park, Marley Park and Sandymount, all less than a 15-minute drive from the city centre. For spectator-driven sports fans, the Shelbourne Park greyhound stadium offers a fun night out and the horse racing at Leopardstown is an institution.

Born-and-bred Dubliners who have lived and worked abroad will tell you that nothing beats the pleasure of returning to the city and the joy of seeing familiar places and catching up with friends. Despite the transformations, some things never change, like the exhilarating summer sunrises over Sandymount Strand, the fresh winds blowing over Dun Laoghaire pier and the swans on the Grand Canal. Perhaps when you come again, Dublin will already feel like home.

DUBLIN IN FIGURES

Geography
- Located at the mouth of the River Liffey on the east coast of Ireland at 53° 20' N – roughly the same latitude as Hamburg, Sheffield, Labrador in Newfoundland and the Queen Charlotte Islands off the west coast of Canada
- 6° 15' W of London, roughly the same longitude as Cadiz in Spain and Rabat in Morocco
- Area: 114sq km

Facts & figures
- The unemployment rate in the first quarter of 2000 was at an all time low in Dublin of 3.9 per cent
- 1,217 divorces were granted in Dublin in 1999. 715 were granted in 1998 and 49 were granted in 1997 – the first year that divorce was legalised in Ireland
- Car ownership in Dublin has increased tenfold from 1996 to 1998
- There was an increase of 44.9 per cent in the total number of new vehicles licensed in February 2000 by comparison with the corresponding month in 1999

Population
- Dublin City and County: April 1999 – 1,096,700 (estimated)
- Dublin City and County: 1991 – 1,025,000 (29.1 per cent of the national total)
- Dublin City and County: 1961 – 719,300
- Approximately 43 per cent of Ireland's population is under 25!

Tourism
- Number of overseas visitors in 1999: 3.4 million
- Increase in visitors between 1998 and 1999: 7 per cent
- Tourism revenue in 1999: IR£561.6 million

Pubs & things
- In 1672 Dublin had 1,180 ale-houses and 93 breweries
- In 1999 there are approximately 850 pubs and only one major brewery
- Like the rest of the Irish people, Dubliners love their potatoes. They eat 48 million tonnes per year

A Chronology

5th century AD	St Patrick converts many of Dublin's inhabitants to Christianity, according to legend.
841	Vikings establish a trading station, probably near present-day Kilmainham.
10th century	Vikings move downstream to the area around Dublin Castle.
1014	High King Brian Boru defeats the Dublin Vikings at the Battle of Clontarf.
1038	Sigtryggr, King of Dublin, founds Christ Church Cathedral.
1172	After Norman barons invade Ireland from Wales, King Henry II gives Dublin to the men of Bristol.
1348	Black Death reaches Dublin and claims one-third of its inhabitants over the next three years.
1592	Queen Elizabeth I grants a charter for the founding of Trinity College.
1680	The Royal Hospital at Kilmainham, the city's first classical building, is begun.
18th century	Dublin's population expands from 40,000 to 172,000.
1712	Work on Trinity College Library begins.
1713	Jonathan Swift is appointed Dean of St Patrick's Cathedral.
1714	Accession of King George I marks the beginning of the Georgian era, Dublin's great period of classical architecture.
1742	Handel conducts the first performance of his *Messiah* in the city's old Musicke Hall.
1745	Building of Leinster House (now home of the Irish Parliament) leads to much new housing development south of the River Liffey.

1759	Arthur Guinness founds the Guinness Brewery.
1760–1800	Dublin reaches the height of its prosperity and architects such as James Gandon create many of the city's fine public buildings.
1782	Irish Parliament secures legislative independence from Britain.
1800	Act of Union is passed and Irish Parliament abolishes itself, prefacing a period of urban decline.
1847	Soup kitchens are set up around Dublin to relieve the effects of the Great Famine.
1854	National Gallery is established.
1916	Easter Rising. The Irish Republic is proclaimed from the General Post Office.
1919	First session of *Dáil Éireann* (Irish Parliament) in the Round Room of the Mansion House.
1922	Civil War declared. After 718 years in residence, British forces evacuate Dublin Castle.
1922	James Joyce's Dublin saga, *Ulysses*, is published in Paris.
1963	President John F Kennedy visits Dublin.
1979	The Pope visits Ireland and says mass in Phoenix Park to over 1.3 million people.
1988	Dublin celebrates its millennium year.
1991	Inauguration of Ireland's first female president, Mary Robinson, at Dublin Castle.
1998	The Good Friday Agreement finally sees a lasting ceasefire to the trouble in the north of Ireland.
2000	The band U2 awarded the Freedom of the City of Dublin.

PEOPLE & EVENTS FROM HISTORY

Photograph of Oscar Wilde taken in 1885

James Joyce

The literary giant most closely associated with Dublin, James Joyce (1882–1941, ➤ 17 and 41), is surprisingly not among its three Nobel-prize-winners (Becket, Shaw and Yeats). Joyce lived and breathed the place, although he always had a love-hate relationship with it. His works in which Dublin appears, almost as a central character, are *A Portrait of the Artist as a Young Man, Ulysses, Dubliners* and *Finnegan's Wake. Ulysses,* his longest work, was originally banned in Ireland when it was first published.

OSCAR WILDE

'Go to Oxford, my dear Oscar: we are much too clever for you over here', said J P Mahaffy in 1874 to his talented student in Trinity College, Dublin. Oscar Wilde (1854–1900) took his advice and left his native city to flaunt his own brand of cleverness, first at Oxford and later in a glittering literary career in *fin de siècle* London. Idolised by London society after the success of his brilliantly epigrammatic plays *Lady Windermere's Fan* (1892) and *The Importance of Being Earnest* (1895), he was later ostracised for committing what was then the crime of homosexuality. After two debilitating years in an English prison, Wilde emigrated to France and died shortly afterwards in Paris.

EASTER RISING

With the founding of the Gaelic League in 1893 and the Abbey Theatre in 1904, the movement for independence gathered momentum in Ireland. Frustrated republicans capitalised on England's preoccupation with World War I to stage a rising in 1916 and declare an independent Republic in Dublin's General Post Office (➤ 37). It was doomed to failure but the execution of several of the insurrection's leaders made rebels out of many Irish royalists, leading five years later to the creation of an Irish Free State. The Republic finally became a reality in 1949.

BRENDAN BEHAN

Author and playwright Brendan Behan stayed in Dublin for most of his comparatively short life although he loved being fêted during his trips to Europe and America. His international reputation was established with *The Quare Fellow* (1954), a play that exposed 'the moral hypocrisy of capital punishment in a society that prides itself on its moral refinement'. An earlier prison sentence for an IRA shooting in 1942 provided material for his first major prose work, *Borstal Boy* (1958). Literature was not Behan's only addiction, and drink led the shouting, singing, swearing darling of Dublin to an early death at the age of 41.

DUBLIN
how to organise your time

13

ITINERARIES

The parts of Dublin worth exploring lie within a fairly compact area bounded by the River Liffey and the city's curvaceous 18th-century canals. To get your bearings, hop on one of the sightseeing buses that circulate regularly. Passengers are free to get off at at one stop and board again later. Once you get a feel of the city, choose one or more of the following itineraries. Book tickets for the theatre (☎ 456 9569) and the Viking Adventure banquet (☎ 490 6077) before you set out.

ITINERARY ONE	ART TOUR
Morning	Take bus No. 7 or 8 from Nassau Street to Lower Mount Street to see the Grand Canal. Walk back to Merrion Square and the Georgian house at 29 Lower Fitzwilliam Street (➤ 47). Cross the square to the National Gallery (➤ 46).
Lunch	Relax in the gallery's restaurant.
Afternoon	Take a northbound bus No. 10 from Clare Street, just round the corner from the gallery, to O'Connell Street. Get off beyond the bridge and walk past the General Post Office toward Parnell Square for the Hugh Lane Gallery (➤ 35) and the Dublin Writers Museum (➤ 36). The James Joyce Centre (➤ 41) is close by.
Evening	Dine at the elegant Tea Rooms (➤ 63) before a performance at The Gate or Abbey Theatre.

ITINERARY TWO	OLD CITY
Morning	Begin the day at University Church (➤ 39) and Newman House (➤ 40). Turn westward towards the medieval part of the city, lured by the spire of St Patrick's Cathedral (➤ 30). Along the way, stop at Marsh's Library (➤ 31).
Lunch	Refuel in the Lord Edward (➤ 66) pub opposite Christ Church Cathedral.
Afternoon	Cross over to Christ Church Cathedral (➤ 29), a stone's throw from Dublin Castle (➤ 34). Have a snack in the castle vaults, then on to the living history museum, the Viking Adventure (➤ 32).
Evening	Banquet in the Viking Adventure.

ITINERARY THREE	**WESTERLY WALK**
Morning	Take bus No. 51B, 78A, 79 or 90 from Aston Quay to Heuston Station or Kilmainham and then walk to the Irish Museum of Modern Art (➤ 25). Leave by the museum's rear gate and follow the path to Kilmainham Gaol (➤ 24).
Lunch	Kilmainham Gaol café.
Afternoon	Continue on to Collins Barracks (➤ 26) then cross over the Liffey to the Guinness Brewery (➤ 50) where you can sample a glass of Dublin's famous brew. Return to the city centre by bus or on foot along the quays.
Evening	Dine in the Temple Bar area.
ITINERARY FOUR	**CULTURE & SHOPPING**
Morning	Start the day in Trinity College Library (➤ 42) to view the magnificent Book of Kells. Leave by the Nassau Street exit and stop briefly at the Heraldic Museum (➤ 43) before moving on to the National Museum (➤ 44).
Lunch	National Museum Café or upstairs in the Kilkenny Design Shop in Nassau Street.
Afternoon	Explore Dublin's poshest shopping district – in and around Nassau Street, Grafton Street (➤ 70) and St Stephen's Green.
Evening	Join a traditional Irish music session (➤ 58) in one of the city's lively pubs.

Always teeming with people, Grafton Street is Dublin's most popular shopping thoroughfare

WALKS

ALONG THE QUAYS WITH GANDON

The English-born architect James Gandon (1743–1823) played an important role in the beautification of Dublin during the late 18th century. This walk begins and ends with his two finest creations. Follow the footpath along the Liffey to see Gandon's impressive buildings reflected in the water.

Start at George's Quay and look across to the Custom House, a magnificent neoclassical building, built by Gandon between 1781 and 1791. At O'Connell Bridge, glance left along Westmoreland Street to see the portico (*c*1784–9) that Gandon added to the Old Parliament House, now the Bank of Ireland (► 38). Continue upstream past the metal bridge, known as the Ha'penny Bridge (1816). At Capel Street Bridge, look south along Parliament Street to Thomas Cooley's City Hall built in 1769, some time before Gandon arrived in Dublin. Turn to admire the seahorses on Grattan Bridge, and Betty Maguire's Viking Boat sculpture (20th century). Continue past the City Offices on your left, where excavations unearthed a Viking site in the 1970s, until you reach Merchant's Quay. Here you have the best view of Gandon's second masterpiece, the Four Courts built between 1786 and 1802 (► 52).

THE SIGHTS

- Custom House (► 52)
- Bank of Ireland (► 38)
- City Hall
- Four Courts (► 52)

INFORMATION

Distance About 2km
Time 45 minutes
Start point George's Quay
⊞ L8
🚉 Tara Street
End point Merchant's Quay
⊞ J9
🚉 None nearby

Gandon's majestic Four Courts, with its Arms of Ireland carved by Edward Smith (inset)

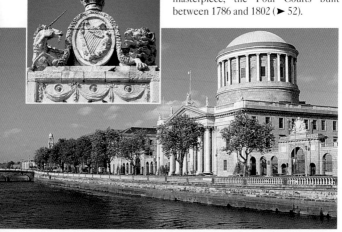

A SHORT JOYCEAN ODYSSEY

In *Ulysses*, James Joyce had his fictional hero, Leopold Bloom, traverse many parts of Dublin during a single day, 16 June, 1904. On the same day every year, enthusiastic costumed Joyceans gather at various points around the city to celebrate the event and retrace their hero's footsteps. To capture some of the Bloomsday spirit, you can follow a small section of the route, indicated by 14 bronze plaques set into the pavement.

The trail starts in Middle Abbey Street at Eason's shop at Nos. 79–80, continues round the corner to Champion Sports (49 O'Connell Street) and then on to the northwest corner of O'Connell Bridge where Bloom experienced 'a puffball of smoke' coming from a barge below. Crossing to the south side of the Liffey, Bloom passed the Ballast Office at the corner of Aston Quay and Westmoreland Street. 'The mockturtle vapour and steam of newbaked jampuffs rolypoly' poured out from Harrison's Restaurant – still there on the east side of Westmoreland Street. Then on to the statue of the poet Thomas Moore (1779–1852), on a triangular traffic island just north of Trinity College. Walk on to the bottom of Grafton Street where Bloom priced field glasses in Messrs Yeats and Sons (now the ICS Building Society) and continue up Grafton Street, past the entrance to Adam Court alleyway, to what was Brown Thomas department store (now on the opposite side of the street). Turn left into Duke Street, stopping at Davy Byrne's and left again into Molesworth Street, where another pub once stood at Nos. 10–11, then on to the final plaque outside the National Museum (➤ 44).

Bronze plaques in the pavement follow the trail of Joyce's Ulysses, starting near O'Connell Street (top)

THE SIGHTS

- O'Connell Bridge
- Statue of Thomas Moore
- Trinity College Library (➤ 42)
- National Museum (➤ 44)
- Grafton Street (➤ 70)

INFORMATION

Distance 1km
Time 45 minutes
Start point Middle Abbey Street (by Eason's shop)
🚇 K8
🚉 Tara Street
End point Kildare Street
🚇 L9
🚉 Pearse

EVENING STROLLS

INFORMATION

Merrion Square & Baggot Street
Distance 2km
Time 40 minutes
Start point Lower Merrion Street
[+] L9
[R] Pearse
[B] 5, 7, 7A, 7X, 8, 45, 84
End point St Stephen's Green
[+] L9
[B] Cross-city buses

Ballsbridge & Donnybrook
Distance 3.5km
Time 60–75 minutes
Start/end point Lansdowne Road
[+] N10
[R] Lansdowne Road
[B] 5, 7, 7A, 7X, 8, 10, 45, 84

Government buildings in Upper Merrion Street

Evening light is kind to Dublin's architecture and under illumination the gently imposing buildings and elegant squares resemble the set of a magnificent period drama.

MERRION SQUARE & BAGGOT STREET

Starting at the Davenport Hotel on Lower Merrion Street enjoy Georgian Dublin by strolling along the north side of Merrion Square. Follow the square along the east side and turn left into Upper Mount Street, before walking down and around St Stephen's Church, returning to admire the bronze figure of the little girl swinging round a Georgian lamp-post. A left turn onto Herbert Street will bring you up to Baggot Street with its lively pubs and restaurants. Turn right and walk towards town. At the point where Baggot Street becomes Merrion Row you can make one of two choices. Turn right down Merrion Street to admire the superbly lit National Gallery and Government buildings before walking back to the Davenport Hotel (your starting place). Alternatively, head straight for Merrion Row to St Stephen's Green.

BALLSBRIDGE & DONNYBROOK

About 2km from the city centre, attractive Ballsbridge is favoured by foreign diplomats and embassies. Starting at Lansdowne Road DART station, head up Shelbourne Road as far as Merrion Road. Cross over and walk to the right of Roly's Bistro to find the entrance to Herbert Park. Walk through the park and perhaps stop to feed the ducks on the centre pond (bring your own bread). Leave via Victoria Avenue before turning left at the end into Donnybrook Road up to the busy crossroads at the Church. Take a left here, then at the next junction turn right into Simmonscourt Road and down to Merrion Road. Once there, head left back towards the city, passing the grounds of the Royal Dublin Society (RDS). There are two good restaurants along this main road, Coopers Café (☎ 660 1525) and Roly's Bistro (☎ 668 2611). Keep along Merrion Road back to Jurys Hotel and Lansdowne Road, where you can catch the DART.

ORGANISED SIGHTSEEING

BY BUS

City tours operate nearly all year round and leave from O'Connell Street. Buy tickets aboard the bus or at Dublin Tourism in Suffolk Street. Dublin Bus ☎ 873 4222; Guide Friday ☎ 676 5377; Irish City Tours ☎ 458 0054; Old Dublin Tours ☎ 670 8822

GUIDED WALKS

Dublin Footsteps   Guided tours start from Bewley's Café, Grafton Street.
☎ 496 0641 🕐 Literary and Georgian Dublin Jun–Oct: daily 11AM
Heart of Dublin Name your own itinerary. Start at Dublin Tourism, Suffolk Street.
☎ 278 1626 🕐 Fri, Sat 10:30AM and 2:30PM
Historic Walking Tour Two hours around the Trinity College area, with university history graduates. Start at the college's front gate.
☎ 845 0241 🕐 May–Sep: Mon–Fri 11, 12, 3; Sun 11, 12, 2, 3
Literary Pub Crawl Visit pubs frequented by literary giants with readings and recitations from Yeats, Joyce, Behan and Beckett. Three hours, starting from the Duke pub, Duke Street.
☎ 454 0228 🕐 Easter–late Oct: daily 7:30PM, Sun noon; Nov–Easter: Thu–Sat 7:30PM, Sun noon
Musical Pub Crawl A tour of Dublin's most popular musical hostelries finishes with a lively musical *seisiún* (musical session, to the unitiated). Starts from the Oliver St John Gogarty pub, Fleet Street.
☎ 478 0191 🕐 May–Oct: Sat–Thu 7:30PM

OTHER WAYS AROUND TOWN

Although not organised sightseeing tours, these are fun ways to get around Dublin.
Horse and Carriage Hire a carriage for a leisurely, if expensive tour, of the city streets and squares. Available almost any time of the day or night.
➕ K9 ✉ Corner Grafton Street and St Stephen's Green
Rickshaw Rides Young Dublin students earn a good living by offering rickshaw rides after dark to anywhere within a 2km radius of Temple Bar.
➕ K9 ✉ Temple Bar

Out-of-Dublin tours

Dublin Bus ☎ 873 4222
Grayline Tours ☎ 670 8822
Mary Gibbons Tours ☎ 283 9973

Kids' special

Viking Splash Tours (➤ 55)

Relaxing on Carolyn Mulholland's bronze tree-shaped chair sculpture (1988), off South Great Georges Street

EXCURSIONS

Malahide Castle – centre-piece of a splendidly wooded estate

INFORMATION

Malahide Castle
Distance About 14km
Travel time 45 minutes
⊞ Off map to northeast
◉ Apr–Oct: Mon–Sat 10–5; Sun and public hols 11–6. Nov–Mar: Mon–Fri 10–5; Sat 2–5; Sun and public hols 2–5
🚌 32, 42
🚆 From Connolly Station to Malahide, then 10-minute walk
ℹ Dublin Tourism ☎ 1850 230 330
❓ Guided tours

Powerscourt
Distance About 25km
Travel time 1 hour
⊞ Off map to southeast
☎ 286 7676
◉ 9:30–5:30 (gardens close at dusk)
🚌 48 to Enniskerry village, then 20-minute walk
🚆 DART to Bray, then feeder bus to Enniskerry
ℹ Dublin Tourism ☎ 1850 230 330
❓ Waterfall inadvisable on foot

MALAHIDE CASTLE

Malahide Castle stands in a large, heavily wooded demesne, some 14km north of Dublin. Apart from one brief interlude during the rule of Oliver Cromwell, the castle remained in the hands of the Talbot family from around 1200 until 1976. The core of the castle is a medieval tower and in the adjoining banqueting hall, the walls are hung with portraits of various members of the Talbot family and other notables. Most of the furnishings are Georgian, chosen to complement the redecoration of much of the interior during the reign of George III (1760–1820).

In a separate building next to the coach park, is the beautifully detailed rolling stock of the Fry Model Railway. Outside, the estate has plenty of opportunities for walking, and the Talbot Botanic Gardens, (May to September) provide a wonderful setting. Created by the late Lord Talbot between 1948 and 1973, they contain exotic plants from Chile, New Zealand and Tasmania.

POWERSCOURT

Careful restoration has converted the 18th-century Palladian mansion into an excellent gallery of shops, with a terrace restaurant. It is set in a dramatic surrounding landscape. To the south, the house looks out over magnificently proportioned stepped terraces, with ornamented sculpture, and a statue throwing a jet of water high in the air. In the distance, the cone-shaped

Landscaped terraces at Powerscourt

INFORMATION

Glendalough
Distance About 50km
Travel time 1 hour 15 minutes

Off map to south

All year: daily. Interpretative center 9:30–5, later in summer

St Kevin's bus departs St Stephen's Green daily 11:30AM. Leaves Glendalough Mon–Sat 4:15PM, Sun 5:30PM

Dublin Tourism ☎ 1850 230 330

Sugar Loaf mountain provides a dramatic backdrop. Gardens stretch to either side; the one to the east is Japanese, the other walled with wrought-iron Bavarian gates. (The story goes that when terraces' designer Daniel Robertson went to inspect the work every morning, he was pushed around in a wheelbarrow. Armed with a full bottle of sherry, he swigged away until he had drained the last drop – his signal to stop work.) You can walk to the waterfall 5km away, but it is easier to get there by car.

Powerscourt waterfall

GLENDALOUGH

Literally the 'valley of two lakes', Glendalough was one of ancient Ireland's most venerated monasteries. Situated at the end of a long valley stretching deep into the Wicklow hills, it grew up around the tomb of its founder, St Kevin, who died in 618. The core of the old monastery consists of a roofless cathedral (c900), a well-preserved Round Tower and St Kevin's Church, roofed with stone. Overlooking the Upper Lake about 2km away is another enchanting church called Reefert. There are good walks in the surrounding woods.

WHAT'S ON

The daily newspapers, both morning and evening, provide good coverage of what's on in Dublin. Pick up a copy of *In Dublin*, printed every two weeks, and look for *The Event Guide*, free from clubs, cafés and restaurants around the capital. Both give listings of events.

January	*Dublin International Theatre Symposium.*
March	*Dublin Film Festival.*
	St Patrick's Festival (14–17 Mar).
	Irish Kennel Club St Patrick's Dog Show at Cloghran, near Dublin Airport.
	St Patrick's Day (17 Mar).
	St Patrick's Festival.
	Dublin Opera Season.
June	*Music Festival* in Great Irish Houses; usually includes a number within easy reach of Dublin.
	Bloomsday (16 Jun), when the hero of James Joyce's novel *Ulysses* is celebrated in word, walks and liquid refreshment (► 17).
	Women's 10-kilometre run.
July	*International Summer School* at University College Dublin.
August	*Kerrygold Dublin Horse Show* in the Royal Dublin Society grounds.
September	*All Ireland Hurling Final.*
	All Ireland Gaelic Football Final.
October	*Dublin Theatre Festival.*
	Wexford Opera Festival, Wexford (129km south).
	Dublin City Marathon.
December	*Dublin Antiques & Fine Arts Fair.*
	National Crafts Fair.
	Christmas Carols in St Patrick's Cathedral (Selected Sundays and special dates).
	Dublin Opera Season.

Buskers in Grafton Street

DUBLIN's
top 25 sights

The sights are shown on the maps on the inside front cover and inside back cover, numbered **1–25** *from west to east across the city*

1

KILMAINHAM GAOL

No escape – chained serpents over the entrance

HIGHLIGHTS

- East wing
- 1916 corridor with cells
- Museum display

INFORMATION

- ✚ F9
- ✉ Inchicore Road, Kilmainham
- ☎ 453 5984
- ⏰ Apr–Sep: daily 9:30–6 (last admission 4:45). Oct–Mar: Mon–Fri 9:30–5 (last admission 4); Sun 10–6 (last admission 4:45)
- 🍴 Café
- 🚉 Heuston
- 🚌 51, 51B, 78A, 79
- ♿ Call in advance for wheelchair assistance
- 👟 Moderate
- ↔ Irish Museum of Modern Art (➤ 25), Collins Barracks (➤ 26)
- ❓ Guided tours only

Leading figures in every rebellion against British rule since 1798 are associated with Kilmainham Gaol and, for many Irish people, their imprisonment or death represents the idea of freedom achieved through sacrifice. Kilmainham has therefore become a potent symbol.

Prisoners A deserted gaol may seem an unusual place to spend a few hours, but with its stark and severe interiors, Kilmainham has a fascination which is more inspirational than morbid. Opened in 1796, and altered frequently since, the gaol is made up of tall interlinked blocks in the centre, flanked by exercise and work yards. During the course of its long history, it held both civil and political prisoners, the earliest of whom were participants in the 1798 rebellion. The flow continued throughout the following century and included the 'Young Ireland' rebels of 1848 (Europe's 'Year of Revolution'), the Fenian suspects of 1867 and notable parliamentarians in the 1880s.

Conditions Overcrowding created appalling conditions when the Great Famine of 1845–9 drove many to petty crime. Closed in 1910, the gaol was reopened during the 1916 rebellion in Dublin to receive insurgents whose execution in the prison in the May and June of that year turned the tide of public opinion in many parts of Ireland in favour of the armed struggle. During the Civil War of the early 1920s, the gaol again housed anti-government rebels including many women, and four Republican leaders were executed. The doors were closed in 1924, and the abandoned gaol was eventually restored by volunteer groups between 1960 and 1984. It is now cared for by the State, which has installed an excellent museum display and other facilities.

IRISH MUSEUM OF MODERN ART

The Royal Hospital at Kilmainham, once a haven for retired soldiers, is now an ultra-modern cultural centre where changing exhibitions showcase the latest trends in contemporary art.

Shelter The most important surviving 17th-century building in Ireland, the Royal Hospital at Kilmainham was founded as the Irish equivalent of the Invalides in Paris and the Chelsea pensioners' hospital in London. The architect, surveyor-general Sir William Robinson, laid out the structure around an open quadrangle, and created a covered arcade around three sides of the ground floor so that residents could stroll outdoors even in inclement weather. Work was completed by 1686, except for the tower and steeple, which were added by Sir Thomas Burgh (► 26) between 1701 and 1704. The doorways at the centre of each side had tympana adorned with military trophies, a rarity in baroque Ireland, but the dining hall and the Chapel (now used for private functions) were the most decorative parts of the whole hospital.

Transformation A hospital until 1922, the building was transformed 70 years later into the National Centre for Culture and the Arts, covering music and, particularly, contemporary art. The Irish Museum of Modern Art possesses its own collections, such as the excellent Madden-Arnholz collection of historic prints (from Dürer onwards) and the New York Portfolio, Gordon Lambert's gift of prints by prominent American artists. Selections from these are frequently on display on the ground and first floors, and the museum regularly stages changing exhibitions of modern art from Europe and beyond.

Royal Hospital steeple

HIGHLIGHTS

- Covered arcade
- Tympana
- Permanent collections
- Visiting exhibitions

INFORMATION

- ✚ G9
- ✉ Royal Hospital, Military Road
- ☎ 612 9900
- 🕐 Tue–Sat 10–5:30; Sun and public hols noon–5:30
- 🍴 Café
- 🚇 Heuston
- 🚌 68, 68A, 69, 78A, 79, 80, 123
- ♿ Good except for East Wing
- 💶 Free; New Gallery moderate
- ↔ Collins Barracks (► 26)
- ❓ Guided tours of exhibitions Wed and Fri 2:30PM; Sat 11:30AM

25

COLLINS BARRACKS

HIGHLIGHTS

- Old barracks building
- Curator's Selection
- Fonthill vase
- Multi-storey clock

INFORMATION

- ✚ H8
- ✉ Benburb Street
- ☎ 677 7444 (ext 405)
- 🕐 Tue–Sat 10–5; Sun 2–5
- 🍴 Café
- 🚇 Heuston
- 🚌 25, 25A, 66, 67, 90
- ♿ Very good, difficult in parts
- 💲 Free
- ⟷ Modern Art Museum (► 25)
- ❓ Book tours in advance

Floral tapestry exhibit

Here in a wonderful new setting you can view the decorative arts and folk life collections of the National Museum – products of Irish artists and craftspeople that have been hidden from view for many years.

The building Sir Thomas Burgh (1670–1730), best known as architect of the Old Library in Trinity College (► 42), also designed Dublin's large Royal Barracks, some 2km outside the city. Built in 1704, on high ground overlooking the River Liffey, they were handed over in 1922 to the Irish State, which named them after Michael Collins, the revolutionary leader killed in an ambush towards the end of the Civil War. Until decommissioning in 1997, they were generally thought to be the oldest military barracks still in use anywhere in the world.

Exhibits The barracks opened as an annexe to the National Museum in the same year, greatly strengthening Dublin's cultural and historical focus. The items on display range from the 17th century to the present day and comprise Irish silver, glass, furniture and costumes, all of which reached a high point of artistic excellence, particularly in the 18th century. Look for some stunning objects from outside Ireland that appear in the 'Curator's Selection', a computerised innovation that gives information about the items at the touch of a screen. Don't miss the Chinese porcelain Fonthill vase, which has managed to survive its well-documented wanderings in Asia and Europe, or the clock whose winding chains extend the height of two floors.

GLASNEVIN

Once the site of a monastery, this leafy suburb has two well-wooded neighbours separated only by a tall stone wall – the National Botanic Gardens and the National Cemetery.

Botanic Gardens Ireland's most extensive and varied collection of plants are carefully tended here. Generously laid out over 19ha, the gardens were founded in 1795, although the Addison Yew walk – named for Joseph Addison, the essayist and wit who used to frequent Glasnevin with Jonathan Swift – must have already been some 50 years old at the time. The curvilinear greenhouses, built by Richard Turner, a Dubliner who created a similar structure for Kew Gardens in London, are among the finest surviving examples of 19th-century glass-and-iron construction. Many of the plants housed within originate from Southeast Asia; one rarity, the handkerchief tree (so called because the whitish leaves enclosing each flower resemble handkerchiefs), comes from China. The rose bush near the entrance was propagated from one in County Kilkenny that inspired Thomas Moore's celebrated poem *The Last Rose of Summer*.

Cemetery The adjoining cemetery is reached by a separate entrance 2km away. Its graves are a *Who's Who* of modern Ireland's formative years: Charles Stewart Parnell, Michael Collins and Eamon de Valera. At the foot of Ireland's tallest Round Tower lie the remains of Daniel O'Connell (1775–1847), who founded the cemetery and liberated Irish Catholics from repressive religious legislation. Kavanagh's pub, outside the old entrance, is known locally as the Grave-diggers'; thirsty grave-diggers would pass their shovels through an opening in its wall and a pint of beer was added to restore their spirits.

HIGHLIGHTS

Botanic Gardens
- Palm house
- Curvilinear glasshouses
- Handkerchief tree
- Last Rose of Summer

Cemetery
- Round tower
- O'Connell's tomb in crypt
- Parnell's grave
- Michael Collins' plot

INFORMATION

Botanic Gardens
- ✛ K5
- ✉ Glasnevin Hill Road
- ☎ 837 4388
- ◐ Summer: Mon–Sat 9–6; Sun 11–6. Winter: daily 11–4:30
- 🚊 Drumcondra
- 🚌 13, 19, 134
- ♿ Good except for some greenhouses
- 💷 Free

Cemetery
- ✛ J5
- ✉ Finglas Road, Glasnevin
- ☎ 830 1133
- ◐ Daily 9–5
- 🍴 Café
- 🚊 Drumcondra
- 🚌 40, 40A
- ♿ Good, except for crypt
- 💷 Free
- ❓ None

Top: Great Palm House of 1884 in the National Botanic Gardens

5

DUBLINIA

HIGHLIGHTS

- Re-creation of medieval Dublin
- Scale model
- Interactive re-created Medieval Fair
- Medieval artefacts
- View over Dublin

INFORMATION

- J9
- St Michael's Hill, Christchurch
- 679 4611
- Apr–Sep: daily 10–5. Oct–Mar: daily 11–4
- 123
- Café
- Dublinia: good. Tower and bridge: none
- Moderate
- Christ Church (➤ 29), Viking Adventure (➤ 32)
- Recorded audio guide

Top & below: medieval Dublin life re-created

If you want to know just what made Dublin's medieval ancestors tick, check out the Dublinia exhibition, a scale model of the medieval city together with tableaus of old city scenes and an audiovisual show.

Vivid re-creation Dublinia, as the town was first recorded on a map c1540, is a colourful re-creation of medieval Dublin life housed in the Victorian-era former Synod Hall. After the Vikings had re-established the city in this area during the 10th century, Hiberno-Norsemen and the Normans occupied it from 1170 until the end of the Middle Ages – the time-span covered by Dublinia.

Excavations One of the most impressive features is the scale model that shows Dublin as it was around 1500. Christ Church Cathedral can be seen inside the city walls and St Patrick's Cathedral beyond. Thirty years of excavations in the Dublinia area have uncovered many fascinating artefacts such as leatherwork, pottery decorated with amusing faces, floor tiles, jewellery and ships' timbers, which are also on view in the exhibition. An audiovisual presentation of the city's history complements the series of life-size model tableaus that illustrate episodes from the past. Climb the 96 steps inside the tower of 15th-century St Michael's Church, incorporated into the Synod Hall when it was built, for great views of the city and the River Liffey. Then cross the enclosed bridge to Christ Church Cathedral, the price of which is included in the Dublinia ticket.

6

CHRIST CHURCH CATHEDRAL

Christ Church Cathedral, the public heart of the city in the Middle Ages, is not only Dublin's oldest stone building but also perhaps the Normans' outstanding contribution to Irish architecture.

Top: 14th-century knight's effigy in the nave

History The older of Dublin's two cathedrals, Christ Church was founded by the Norse king Sigtryggr Silkenbeard in 1038. The northern side of the choir and the south transept are the oldest parts of the existing stone structure and have been dated back to just before 1180, indicating that the Normans started the building shortly after they took over the city, using masons brought over from the west of England. The early Gothic nave, dated *c*1226–36, also reflects English influence. Its vault collapsed in 1562, leaving the north wall with a remarkable outward lean of about half a metre.

Restoration The whole building would now be a romantic ivied ruin but for the intervention of the Dublin whiskey distiller Henry Roe, who paid for its reconstruction between 1872 and 1878. The work was carried out under the direction of the great English Victorian architect George Edmund Street, who added flying buttresses to keep the whole edifice standing. Look for the effigy of a knight in armour near the entrance, traditionally thought to represent the great Norman knight, Strongbow (Robert de Clare). In the Peace Chapel of Saint Laud is the heart-reliquary of the cathedral's co-founder, Saint Laurence O'Toole, who died in Normandy in 1180. An unusual feature is the original crypt, which extends the entire length of the cathedral. Here you can see 17th-century statues from another Dublin building and a mummified cat and rat, trapped in a fateful chase through an organ pipe.

HIGHLIGHTS

- 12th-century south transept
- Leaning north wall
- Knight's effigy
- Crypt
- Mummified cat and rat

INFORMATION

- ✚ J9
- ✉ Christ Church Place
- ☎ 677 8099
- 🕐 Daily 10–5, except during Sun service
- 🚉 Tara Street
- ♿ None
- 💷 Voluntary (IR£1 suggested)
- ↔ Dublinia (➤ 28), St Patrick's (➤ 30), Marsh's Library (➤ 31), Viking Adventure (➤ 32)
- ❓ Occasional tours or book in advance

7

ST PATRICK'S CATHEDRAL

Top: monument of Archbishop Thomas Jones (c1620).
Above: the nave

HIGHLIGHTS

- Swift's bust and epitaph
- Medieval brasses
- Memorial to Carolan
- Organ
- Living Stones Exhibition

INFORMATION

- ✚ J9
- ✉ St Patrick's Close
- ☎ 475 4817
- 🕐 Mon–Fri 9–6; Sat 9–5
  (Nov–Mar: 9–4); Sun
  10–11, 12:15–3 (Nov–Apr:
  10:30–11, 12:45–3)
- 🚉 Tara Street
- 🚌 65B, 77
- ♿ None
- 💷 Moderate
- ↔ Marsh's Library (➤ 31),
  Christ Church (➤ 29)

'Here is laid the body of Jonathan Swift, Doctor of Divinity, Dean of this Cathedral Church, where fierce indignation can no longer rend the heart. Go traveller, and imitate, if you can, this earnest and dedicated champion of liberty.'

Literary connections Jonathan Swift's epitaph is a fitting tribute to the personality most often associated with St Patrick's Cathedral. The author of *Gulliver's Travels* – originally written as a political satire but equally enjoyed by generations of children – Swift was the cathedral's fearless and outspoken Dean from 1713 until his death in 1745. He and his beloved Stella, rumoured to have been his wife, are buried just inside the modern entrance.

History Founded as a church in 1192, and raised to cathedral status in 1219, St Patrick's was built in the early English Gothic style and completed by 1284. The fact that Dublin has two Protestant cathedrals is something of a paradox in a predominantly Catholic city and country. Like Christ Church (➤ 29), St Patrick's was heavily restored in the 19th century, entirely with funds from the wealthy Guinness family.

Flags The monuments in the cathedral and on its walls include the tomb and effigy of the 17th-century adventurer Richard Boyle, Earl of Cork, and a memorial to great Irish bard and harpist Turlough Carolan (1670–1738). In the south choir aisle are two of Ireland's rare 16th-century monumental brasses. The flags in the north transept were carried by Irish regiments, who experienced both victory and tragedy in battle; those in the choir commemorate the noble order of the Knights of St Patrick. The cathedral organ is the largest in Ireland.

MARSH'S LIBRARY

A magnificent example of an 18th-century scholar's library, Marsh's Library has changed little since it opened nearly 300 years ago. One of the few buildings in Dublin to retain its original purpose, it remains a calm oasis of scholarly learning.

Rare legacy In 1701, Archbishop Narcissus Marsh (1638–1713) built Ireland's first public library close to St Patrick's Cathedral and filled it with his own books and 10,000 others purchased in 1705 from the Bishop of Worcester. Two years later, it was given official legal standing when the Irish parliament passed an Act for 'settling and preserving a public library'. The building is one of the city's rare legacies from the reign of Queen Anne and was designed by Sir William Robinson, responsible for the Royal Hospital at Kilmainham (▶ 25), using distinctive grey Dublin limestone on one side and red brick on the front.

Precious books Inside, the long gallery is flanked on each side by dark oak bookcases adorned with carved and lettered gables topped by carvings of an archbishop's mitre. At the end of the L-shaped gallery are three alcoves or 'cages' where readers were locked with the library's precious books. As an extra safeguard, chains were attached to the books (though not to the readers). The volumes reflect the founder's wide-ranging interests, and the oldest example is Cicero's *Letters to his Friends*, published in Milan in 1472. The library also possesses some 300 manuscripts, displayed with other items in glass-fronted cases.

HIGHLIGHTS

- Old-world atmosphere
- Oak bookcases
- 'Cages' for rare works
- Books and manuscripts

INFORMATION

- ✚ J9
- ✉ St Patrick's Close
- ☎ 454 3511
- 🕐 Mon, Wed, Thu, Fri 10–12:45, 2–5; Sat 10:30–12:45
- 🚉 Tara Street
- 🚌 65B, 77
- ♿ None
- 💷 Moderate
- ↔ Dublinia (▶ 28), St Patrick's (▶ 30), Christ Church (▶ 29)
- ❓ Group tours by arrangement

Alcoves lined with leather-bound tomes

9

VIKING ADVENTURE

HIGHLIGHTS

- Reconstructed Viking houses
- Simulated boat trip
- Excavation panorama
- Partial Viking ship reconstruction
- Original Viking artefacts
- Small laboratory

INFORMATION

- ✚ K9
- ✉ Essex Street West, Temple Bar
- ☎ 679 6040
- 🕐 Tue–Sat 10–4:30
- 🚆 Tara Street
- 🚌 37, 70, 39, 67, 67A, 51B
- ♿ Good
- 💷 Expensive
- ↔ Christ Church (➤ 29), Dublinia (➤ 28)
- ❓ Tours every 30 mins (lasts 45 mins)

The Vikings received a bad press even before the Irish king Brian Boru defeated them in 1014. It was only when the City Fathers planned to destroy their remains in 1978 that the citizens of Dublin rallied to their defence and made them heroes.

Viking skills The city of Dublin owes its origins to the Vikings, Scandinavia's Northmen, who started a trading colony upriver from the centre in 841 before moving in the 10th century to a new settlement in the area around Christ Church Cathedral. Here excavations have uncovered their well-preserved wattle-and-timber houses and evidence of their craftsmanship in bone, leather and metalwork. Through their navigational and commercial skills, the Vikings transformed Dublin into a marketplace of international repute, and introduced Ireland to the benefits of coinage and maritime towns.

Layers The Viking Adventure celebrates this huge contribution to the city's early development. The 'experience' begins with a simulated ocean voyage aboard a Viking ship bound for Dyflin (Viking Dubin). Here life-sized reconstructions of typical Viking houses, and costumed actors regaling colourful tales, bring everything to life. A deconsecrated church is pressed into service to re-create a section of an archaeological dig. Its ramped walkways zigzag upward, so that you can see the various strata of the excavation, from the lower Viking layers through those of later eras closer to ground level. A stunning replica of a great Viking ship provides a backdrop for evening banquets (➤ 58). At the end of your tour, you can view displays of actual Viking finds excavated from a nearby site, together with a small laboratory equipped with the tools and materials needed to preserve the artefacts.

Top: the Viking era brought to life

CHESTER BEATTY LIBRARY & GALLERY

Sir Alfred Chester Beatty is one of the few people to have been made an honorary citizen of Ireland. For giving the nation such rare and priceless art collections, he richly deserved this award.

Hidden treasure The library and oriental art gallery named after its founder and benefactor, Sir Alfred Chester Beatty (1875–1968), is one of Dublin's greatest jewels yet one that many visitors have unwittingly ignored. The collection has been transferred to a more accessible home in a converted Georgian building next to Dublin Castle (▶ 34). A more fitting home for such a trove of treasures.

Masterpieces Alfred Chester Beatty, a successful mining engineer born in New York and knighted for his services to Britain as an advisor to Winston Churchill during World War II, devoted an important part of his life to the search for manuscripts and *objets d'art* of the highest quality. The collections range from *c*2700 BC up to the 19th century, and stretch geographically from Japan in the east to Europe in the west. Religious writings range from one of the earliest known New Testament papyri to the Korans, all masterpieces of calligraphy. There is a wealth of Persian and Mughal miniature paintings as well as wonders of the East such as Burmese and Siamese painted fairytale books or *parabaiks*, Chinese silk paintings and jade snuff bottles, and Japanese netsuke and woodblock prints. Exhibitions are focused on two diverse themes – Great Religions of the World and Secular Arts and Patronage.

Top: Chinese ceiling in the old Library
Right: Oriental art exhibit

HIGHLIGHTS

- New Testament papyri
- Koran manuscripts
- Persian and Mughal paintings
- Jade snuff bottles

INFORMATION

- ✚ K9
- ✉ Clock Tower, Dublin Castle
- ☎ 269 2386
- 🕐 Tue–Sat 10–5; Sun 2–5
- 🍴 Café
- 🚉 Tara Street
- 🚌 50, 54A, 56 , 77
- Good
- ♿ Free (charge for special events)
- ↔ Dublinia (▶ 28), St Patrick's Cathedral (▶ 30), Christ Church Cathedral (▶ 29), Dublin Castle (▶ 34), Viking Adventure (▶ 32)
- ❓ Audiovisual. Guided tours

DUBLIN CASTLE

HIGHLIGHTS

- Powder Tower
- State Apartments
- Chapel Room

INFORMATION

- ✚ K9
- ✉ Dame Street/Castle Street
- ☎ 677 7129
- ◷ Mon–Fri 10–12:15, 2–5; Sat, Sun and public hols 2–5
- 🍴 Restaurant
- 🚇 Tara Street
- 🚌 50, 54A, 56, 77
- ♿ State Apartments: good Powder Tower: none
- 📷 Varies
- ↔ Christ Church (➤ 29), Viking Adventure (➤ 32)
- ❓ Chapel Royal and gardens, open Mon–Fri, do not form part of tour

The Throne Room in the State Apartments

How many buildings in Europe can claim to have been the centre of a country's secular power for longer than Dublin Castle, which was the headquarters of English rule in Ireland for over 700 years?

Ancient site Dublin Castle, now used for State occasions, presidential inaugurations and occasional European summit meetings, stands on the site of a much older Viking settlement. It occupies the southeastern corner of the Norman walled town, overlooking the long-vanished black pool or *dubh linn* that gave the city its ancient Irish name. The castle's defined rectangular shape was determined from the start in 1204 with the construction of a twin-towered entrance on the north side and stout circular bastions at each corner. The excavated remains of one of these, the Powder Tower, shown on the guided tour, rested on an earlier Viking foundation and was attached to the city wall beside an arch, beneath which water flowed from the old castle moat.

Interior After a disastrous fire in 1684, the interior was almost entirely rebuilt in the 18th and early 19th centuries. On the south side of Upper Castle Yard are the State Apartments, where the English king's viceroy lived until the castle was ceremoniously handed over to the Irish State in 1922. These regal rooms form the second half of the guided tour, which starts in the Powder Tower.

HUGH LANE GALLERY

Degas, Monet, Corot and Renoir are among the Impressionist artists whose paintings are on display in this wonderful gallery that also looks back over a hundred years of the Irish arts.

Philanthropist The Hugh Lane Gallery of Modern Art fills a niche between the old Masters on display in the National Gallery (► 46) and the ultramodern creations in the Irish Museum of Modern Art at Kilmainham (► 25). Built between 1761 and 1763 by the Earl of Charlemont to the designs of Sir William Chambers (► 48), the gallery now bears the name of Sir Hugh Lane who was drowned when the *Lusitania* sank off the Cork coast in 1915. Before his death, Sir Hugh added a codicil to his will stating that a group of 39 of his Impressionist pictures that were then in London, including works by Corot, Degas, Manet, Monet and Renoir, should go to Dublin. However, the codicil remained unwitnessed with the result that London claimed the canvases and kept them until it was agreed that each city should display half of them at any one time in rotation. The latest coup is the Francis Bacon studio, bequeathed to the gallery on the artist's death.

Modern art Irish artists of the last hundred years, including Osborne, Yeats, Orpen, Henry and Le Brocquy, are also well represented; modern European artists include Beuys and Albers. An exhibition of paintings by Roderic O'Connor (1860–1940) will remain in place until 2002. Make sure you see the stunning examples of stained glass by Clarke, Home and Scanlon.

HIGHLIGHTS

- Impressionist paintings
- Jack Yeats, *There is no night*
- Orpen, *Homage to Manet*
- Works by Roderic O'Connor
- Stained glass
- Francis Bacon's studio (opening May 2001)

INFORMATION

- 🔲 K7
- ✉ Parnell Square North
- ☎ 874 1903
- ⏰ Tue–Thu 9:30–6; Fri, Sat 9:30–5; Sun 11–5
- 🚉 Connolly
- 🚌 Cross-city buses
- ♿ Few
- 🎫 Free
- ↔ Dublin Writers Museum (► 36), James Joyce Centre (► 41)

Augustus John's 1920 portrait of Miss Iris Tree

13

DUBLIN WRITERS MUSEUM

HIGHLIGHTS

- Letters of Thomas Moore and Maria Edgeworth
- Yeats manuscript
- Indenture signed by Swift
- Busts of George Bernard Shaw and Oscar Wilde

INFORMATION

- ✚ K7
- ✉ 18 Parnell Square North
- ☎ 872 2077
- 🕓 Mon–Sat 10–5; Sun and public hols 11–5. Late opening Jun–Aug: 10–6
- 🍴 Café
- 🚉 Connolly Station
- 🚌 Cross-city buses
- ♿ None
- 💷 Moderate
- ↔ Hugh Lane Gallery (➤ 35), James Joyce Centre (➤ 41)
- ❓ Recorded audio guide

For centuries a meeting point for gifted writers, Dublin has become the centre of a great literary tradition. This museum celebrates their diverse talents and displays a truly fascinating range of memorabilia.

Great Irish writers Many languages have been spoken by Ireland's inhabitants down the centuries, including Norse, Irish and Norman French, but it was with the establishment of English as the *lingua franca* in the 17th century that Dublin's literary reputation was established. Restoration dramatists such as George Farquhar were followed 50 years later by the brilliance and acerbic wit of Jonathan Swift. One hundred years ago, a new era dawned with the emergence of Oscar Wilde, whose elegant epigrams enthralled the world. Around the turn of the century, William Butler Yeats, encouraged by the flourishing Irish literary movement, helped found the Abbey Theatre, which opened in 1904. Since then, Irish writers such as George Bernard Shaw, James Joyce, Samuel Beckett and Brendan Behan have continued to open up new horizons in world literature.

Displays Photographs, paintings and other items linked with Ireland's literary titans are backed up with lots of explanatory material. First editions and rare volumes abound, and there are original letters of the poet Thomas Moore and the 19th-century novelist Maria Edgeworth, a manuscript of W B Yeats and an indenture signed by Jonathan Swift. As well as bronze busts of George Bernard Shaw and Oscar Wilde, the museum has portraits of celebrated and lesser-known artists. Take time to look at the house itself – the stucco work is one example of the craftsmanship used in the 18th-century homes of Dublin's wealthy.

Top: the first-floor portrait gallery of many famous authors who have graced the Dublin scene

GENERAL POST OFFICE

The General Post Office symbolises the birthplace of modern Ireland. Overlooking one of Europe's widest thoroughfares, it was the city's last great public building created in the neoclassical style.

Classical splendour The imposing breadth of O'Connell Street to the north of the River Liffey was the brainchild of the Wide Street Commissioners in the second half of the 18th century – a prescient decision given the volume of today's traffic. The street's focal point was Nelson's Pillar, a Doric column surmounted by the victor of Trafalgar. At a height of 41m, it provided the city's best vantage point until it was toppled by an explosion in 1966. Now the only remnants of the street's once classical splendour are the exterior walls of the General Post Office, designed by Francis Johnston (1814–18). The Ionic portico extends over the footpath at the front, and John Smith's statues of *Hibernia* (with spear and harp), *Mercury* (with a purse) and *Fidelity* dominate the skyline.

Easter Rising Inside the north entrance is a plaque with beautifully cut letters recording the reading of the Proclamation of the Irish Republic in the building during the Easter Rising of 1916. The insurgents were forced to surrender after the interior was reduced to rubble (the bullet chips on the portico columns are a sobering reminder of the bitter struggle) and were later executed. However, their stand led inexorably to the creation of modern Ireland and a salute is given here in their memory at Dublin's annual St Patrick's Day parade.

HIGHLIGHTS

- Ionic portico decoration
- Statues above portico
- Plaques inside entrances

INFORMATION

- ⊞ K8
- ✉ O'Connell Street
- ☎ 705 7000
- ◷ Mon–Sat 8AM–8PM; Sun 10–6:30
- 🚉 Tara Street
- 🚌 Cross-city buses
- ♿ Few
- 💷 Free
- ↔ Hugh Lane Gallery (➤ 35), Dublin Writers Museum (➤ 36), James Joyce Centre (➤ 41)
- ❓ None

Oliver Sheppard's statue of the Dying Cuchulainn *(1911–1912) commemorates the 1916 Rising*

15

BANK OF IRELAND

Cleverly stitched together by various hands over more than six decades, this great semicircular building was once the focus of Ireland's glorious years of freedom at the end of the 18th century, when the city reached the zenith of its architectural and artistic achievement.

Edward Smyth's statue of Liberty over Gandon's east portico (1785–1789)

HIGHLIGHTS

- Exterior detail
- Former House of Lords
- Jan van Beaver tapestries
- Chandelier
- Fireplace

INFORMATION

- K9
- College Green
- 677 7801
- Mon–Fri 10–4 (House of Lords open most days); Thu 10–5
- Tara Street
- Cross-city buses
- Few
- Free
- Trinity College Library (➤ 42)
- Frequent lectures in House of Lords Tue 10:30, 11:30, 1:45

Harmony The Bank of Ireland, overlooking College Green, began life as the upper and lower houses of the old Irish Parliament, which gained its legislative independence in 1782 but saw its members bribed to vote itself out of existence 18 years later. Its first architect was the young Edward Lovett Pearce, who designed the recessed south-facing 'piazza' of Ionic columns (c1729–39) and the rooms behind it, of which the old House of Lords is still intact and frequently made accessible to the public. In it hangs a wonderful Dublin crystal chandelier (1788) of 1,233 pieces, and two fine tapestries (1733) by Jan van Beaver – one of King James II at the 1689 Siege of Londonderry, the other of King William of Orange astride his steed at the 1690 Battle of the Boyne. The fireplace in the north wall of the room is the work of a Dublin carver, Thomas Oldham.

Alterations The architect James Gandon (➤ 16) added the curving and windowless screen and the east-facing Corinthian portico between 1785 and 1789, and a corresponding portico was added to the west side some years later. After the parliament was dissolved, the building was sold in 1802 to the Bank of Ireland, on condition that it be modified to prevent it from being used again for public debate. These changes were carried out by Francis Johnston, whose work forms the basis of the contemporary banking rooms.

UNIVERSITY CHURCH

This Byzantine-style church has to be one of Dublin's most unusual ecclesiastical edifices; the only building where Cardinal John Henry Newman left an architectural record of his presence in the capital.

Vision Convert, champion of intellectual freedom, and one of the world's first ecumenists, Newman (1801–90) spent the years 1854 to 1858 in Dublin. While he was in the process of setting up what he hoped would be the 'Catholic University of the English tongue for the whole world' (► 40), he acquired the garden plot between Nos. 86 and 87 St Stephen's Green and set about building a church to promote his ideals. Jutting out onto the pavement is the porch, which through a later addition, has carved capitals of early Christian design that suggest the Byzantine splendour within.

Byzantine interior In the nave, the richly coloured Irish marble slabs panelling the side walls are particularly striking, and frame a niche containing a bust of Newman by Thomas Farrell. Look for the attractive little birds on the capitals of the columns dividing the marble panels. John Hungerford Pollen, an architect and friend of Newman, came over from England to supervise the building. Pollen also painted the ceiling and executed the wonderful golden apse decorated with a tree of life with various echoes of medieval Flemish figures and the architecture of an ancient Roman basilica. After its completion in 1856, Newman described the church as 'the most beautiful one in the three Kingdoms'.

HIGHLIGHTS

- Marble panelling
- Carved birds on capitals
- Ceiling
- Golden apse

INFORMATION

✚	K10
✉	86–7 St Stephen's Green
☎	478 0616/475 118
🕐	Mon–Sat 9–5:30; Sun 10–1, 5–6
🍴	Restaurant at No. 86
🚌	Cross-city buses
🚆	Pearse
♿	None
💷	Free
◉	Newman House (► 40)

Byzantine splendour

17

NEWMAN HOUSE

Apollo *in stucco by the Lafranchini brothers*

INFORMATION

🞣 K10
✉ 85–86 St Stephen's Green
☎ 706 7422
🕐 Jun–Sep: Tue–Fri 10– 4:30; Sat 2–4:30; Sun 11–4
🍴 Café
🚶 Pearse
🚌 Cross-city buses
♿ None
📖 Moderate
↔ University Church (➤ 39)
❓ Guided tours only, on the hour, except 1PM

The exuberant stucco work of this house on St Stephen's Green provided the baroque and rococo background to nurture the literary genius of John Henry Newman, Gerard Manley Hopkins and James Joyce.

Ornamentation Named after one of the 19th-century's greatest liberal intellectuals, Newman House is actually two great houses. No. 85 was built in 1738 for Captain Hugh Montgomery, a member of Parliament wealthy enough to employ Switzerland's great Lafranchini brothers to decorate the walls and ceilings with stucco ornament. Their most notable achievements are the figures of Apollo and the nine muses on the ground floor, and the extravagant ceiling of the Saloon, which stretches the entire length of the first floor.

Experiment In 1754, another parliamentarian, Richard Chapel Whaley, bought No. 85 and just over ten years later, built the house at No. 86. The interior here is embellished with equally exuberant stucco work, particularly the stair-case. Whaley's religious intolerance contrasted sharply with the ethos of Cardinal Newman, who used the mansion in the 1850s for his great experiment in bringing education to the Catholic masses – a liberal Victorian university. Called the Catholic University of Ireland, it was intended as a rival to the long-established Protestant Trinity College. On the top floor is the room once occupied by Gerard Manley Hopkins, a Jesuit priest and fellow-countryman; one of the founders of modern poetry, he was professor of classics at the college from 1884 to 1889. Later alumni included James Joyce, who studied here between 1899 and 1902.

JAMES JOYCE CENTRE

Of all the literati to grace the Dublin scene during the 20th century, James Joyce has undoubtedly earned the greatest reputation internationally, so it is fitting that a whole house is devoted to the writer and his work.

HIGHLIGHTS

- Joyce family members
- Recordings
- Library
- Portraits of characters in *Ulysses*
- Door from No. 7 Eccles Street

Connections This 18th-century house, in an impressive street of equally well-restored Georgian redbrick residences just 275m from O'Connell Street, is home to the James Joyce Centre. Initially, its Joycean connection was established through a dapperly dressed dancing master called Denis J Maginni, who leased one of the rooms in the house around the turn of the century and appears as a character in *Ulysses*. A more immediate connection is the presence of members of the novelist's family, including his nephew Ken Monaghan, who show visitors around the house and give them the opportunity to listen to tapes of Uncle James reading from *Ulysses* and *Finnegan's Wake*.

Jacques Emile Blanche's portrait of James Joyce

Memorabilia Take time out to browse in the extensive library and gaze at the portraits of those featured in the master's work, either under their own name or a pseudonym. You can also see the original doorway rescued from the now-demolished No. 7 Eccles Street, the imagined residence of the Ulyssean hero, Leopold Bloom, as you head for the small café at the back of the house. The centre is also a starting point for an hour-long walking tour (payable separately) of Joycean sites on the north side of the city.

INFORMATION

- ✠ K7
- ✉ 35 North Great Georges Street
- ☎ 878 8547
- 🕔 9:30–5; Sun 12:30–5
- 🍴 Café open in summer
- 🚆 Connolly
- 🚌 Cross-city buses
- ♿ Few
- 💷 Moderate
- ↔ Writers Museum (➤ 36)
- ❓ Guided tours of house and surrounding area

41

19

TRINITY COLLEGE LIBRARY

HIGHLIGHTS

- Book of Kells
- Book of Durrow
- Book of Armagh
- Audiovisual 'Dublin Experience'

INFORMATION

- K9
- College Green
- 608 2308
- Oct–May: Mon–Sat 9–5; Sun noon–4:30. Jun–Sep: Mon–Sat 9:30–5; Sun 9:30–4:30
- Café on campus
- Pearse
- Cross-city buses
- Good
- Moderate
- College tours May–Sep

A page from the Book of Kells (c800)

Here you will find one of the most joyously decorative manuscripts of the first Christian millennium, the Book of Kells, one of the greatest creations of Western art. Arrive early, especially in summer, for the best view.

Surroundings An oasis of fresh air, Trinity College is also the noblest assemblage of classical buildings in the city. Inside, the open square marked with Arnoldo Pomodoro's sculpture *Sphere within Sphere* (1982–3) is surrounded on three sides by some of Dublin's finest modern and ancient buildings – Paul Koralek's New Library (1978) to the south, Benjamin Woodward's splendidly carved Museum building (1853–5) to the east and Thomas Burgh's dignified Old Library (1712–32) to the west. In 1857, Woodward altered Burgh's building and made its barrel-vaulted upper floor into one of Ireland's most breathtaking spaces – lined with books from floor to ceiling and handsomely decorated with marble busts of Jonathan Swift and others.

Book of Kells The library is an appropriate setting for Ireland's greatest collection of medieval manuscripts. Among these, pride of place goes to the Book of Kells (c800), a Gospel book that has been bound in four separate sections so that its brilliantly ornamented pages and text may be viewed side by side. Displayed alongside are the important books of Durrow (c700) and Armagh (c800), the latter giving us most of the information we have about Ireland's patron saint, Patrick. The exhibition in the Old Library's main chamber gives useful background information on the collections.

HERALDIC MUSEUM

Every year, thousands of people come to Ireland in search of their roots, but even those without a drop of Irish blood will find this museum fascinating, both in its contents and context.

Heraldry The Heraldic Museum, an integral part of the National Library, is housed in Dublin's most colourful mid-19th-century building – the former Kildare Street Club (1858–61), designed by Benjamin Woodward. (The decorative birds and amusing monkeys playing billiards and musical instruments among the window carvings are enough to make a visit worthwhile.) The museum occupies the club's former dining-room, beneath the tall ceiling of which hang modern banners of Ireland's ancient chieftain families. Needless to say, heraldry is everywhere – on the livery buttons of gentlemen's servants, on the crest of the Joyce clan of Galway, or embellishing items of 19th-century Belleek pottery bearing the coats of arms of Irish towns. Look for the colours of the Irish infantry regiments who fought in France during the 18th century as well as the mantle and insignia of the knightly Order of St Patrick.

Napoleon Despite the emphasis on Irish family history, there are also objects from outside Ireland. You will find the arms of the city of Cologne, along with those of the Spencer-Churchill family (late 18th-century), Napoleon Bonaparte and Sir Francis Drake. The 14th-century crusader badge made of pewter is another intriguing item. If you are inspired to trace your own Irish ancestry, enquire at the Consultancy Service of the National Library, just a few doors along from the museum.

HIGHLIGHTS

- Animal sculptures on façade
- Banners of Irish Chieftains
- Colours of Irish infantry in France
- Arms of Napoleon
- Heraldic Insignia Exhibition

INFORMATION

- 🚻 L9
- ✉ 2–3 Kildare Street
- ☎ 603 0300
- 🕐 Museum: Mon–Wed 10–8:30; Thu, Fri 10–4:30; Sat 10:30–12:30
- 🚆 Pearse
- 🚌 Cross-city buses
- 🚳 None
- 🆓 Free
- ↔ National Museum (▶ 44)

Top: decorative façade

NATIONAL MUSEUM

INFORMATION

- L9
- Kildare Street
- 677 7444
- Tue–Sat 10–5; Sun 2–5
- Café
- Pearse
- Cross-city buses
- Ground floor good
- Free
- Heraldic Museum (➤ 43), Natural History Museum (➤ 45), National Gallery (➤ 46)

The 8th-century Ardagh Chalice in the Treasury Room

Most of Ireland's greatest treasures are housed in the National Museum. A visit here is a must if you want a deeper understanding of the country's history and culture since prehistoric times.

Extensive collections For over a century, the twin institutions of the National Museum (1890) and the National Library have faced each other across the square leading to the *Dáil*, or Houses of Parliament. On the ground floor, the museum displays western Europe's most extensive collection of prehistoric gold ornaments, mostly dating from the Bronze Age (c1500–500 BC). These strikingly shaped pieces of glittering personal adornment were made from thin sheet or massive gold. Even more significant are the brooches, chalices, crosses and croziers (AD 600–1200), largely the products of Ireland's early Christian monasteries, on show in the Treasury Rooms. Among the greatest gems in this dazzling collection are the 8th-century Tara Brooch and Ardagh Chalice, and the 12th-century processional Cross of Cong.

Tribute Another room on the ground floor pays tribute to the participants of the 1916 insurrection, which played such a seminal role in the creation of modern Ireland. Not to be missed upstairs are the contrasting exhibitions on pharaonic Egypt and Viking Dublin, the latter recalling the life and activity of the capital city during the early centuries.

22

NATURAL HISTORY MUSEUM

The old-fashioned glass cases and creaking floorboards have changed little since the inauguration of the museum in 1857, when Dr David Livingstone delivered the opening lecture on his 'African discoveries'.

Fauna The Natural History Museum is one of the four great national institutions flanking the Irish Houses of Parliament. The nucleus of its collection was assembled by the Royal Dublin Society long before it opened, and it has bene-fited greatly from subsequent gifts. Facing you as you enter is the skeleton of the giant Irish deer, better known as the Irish elk, with its impressive antlers. Beyond, is a great array of Irish furred and feathered animals as well as marine species ranging from the greater spotted dogfish and the exotic sunfish to giant lobsters.

Dodo The upper floor is given over to animals of the world, among them the great Irish wolf-hound and a mighty 20-m long whale suspended from the ceiling. There is also a skeleton of the flightless dodo and a cluster of hummingbirds. Geology is something of a sideline but is repre-sented by a meteorite that landed in 1810 on County Tipperary in central Ireland and took some two hours to cool down. A different kind of curios-ity is the outfit worn by Surgeon-Major Thomas Heazle Parke (1858–93), of the Royal Army Medical Corps, who became the first Irishman to cross Africa from coast to coast. The explorer Sir Henry Morton Stanley contributed generously to Parke's statue in front of the museum.

HIGHLIGHTS

- Giant Irish elk
- Great Irish wolfhound
- Fin whale
- Dodo skeleton
- Hummingbird
- Small meteorite

INFORMATION

- ✚ L9
- ✉ Merrion Street
- ☎ 677 7444
- 🕐 Tue–Sat 10–5; Sun 2–5
- 🚉 Pearse
- 🚌 7, 8, 10
- ♿ Ground floor access only
- 💷 Free
- ↔ National Gallery (➤ 46), Number Twenty Nine (➤ 47)

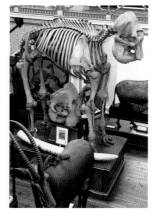

Top & right: skeletons of the past on display

23

NATIONAL GALLERY

Ireland's National Gallery enjoys considerable standing on the international scene as the home of one of Europe's premier collections of Old Masters.

HIGHLIGHTS

- Yeats Museum
- Fra Angelico, *Attempted Martyrdom of SS Cosmas and Damian*
- G David, *Christ Bidding Farewell to His Mother*
- Titian, *Ecce Homo*
- Caravaggio, *The Taking of the Christ*
- Vermeer, *Lady Writing a Letter*
- Rembrandt, *Rest on the Flight into Egypt*
- Picasso, *Still Life with Mandolin*
- Canova, *Amorino*

INFORMATION

- L9
- Merrion Square West
- 661 5133
- Mon–Sat 10–5:30; Thu 10–8:30; Sun 2–5
- Self-service restaurant
- Pearse
- 7, 8, 10
- Very good
- Voluntary
- Natural History Museum (➤ 45), Number Twenty Nine (➤ 47)
- Public tours Sat 3PM; Sun 2:15, 3 and 4PM. Telephone for lectures

Origins Facing on to Merrion Square, and looking across Leinster Lawn at the Natural History Museum (➤ 45), the National Gallery is set in relaxing green surroundings. The gallery was established in 1854, and opened in 1864 to display Old Master paintings as an inspiration to budding Irish artists of the mid-Victorian period. Its contents have expanded twenty-fold in the century-and-a-half since then, helped by numerous bequests. These include works by Vermeer, Velázquez and Murillo (bequeathed by Lady and Sir Alfred Beit, nephew of the co-founder of De Beers); the legacy of one-third of George Bernard Shaw's residual estate enabled the Gallery to acquire important works by Fragonard and J L David, among others.

Masterpieces The Irish paintings, on the ground floor, show a progression from the 18th century onward, while the Old Masters for which the Gallery is famous are on the next floor. A wide coverage is given to most European schools of painting – including icons, early Italians (Uccello and Fra Angelico), Renaissance (Titian, Tintoretto), Dutch and Flemish (G David, Rembrandt, Rubens), early German (Cranach), Spanish (Goya), French (Poussin) and British (Reynolds and Raeburn, among others). The display also covers Impressionists and modern painters up to Picasso. A special room is devoted to watercolours and drawings – including 31 by Turner on display every year in January. There is also a special museum dedicated to the life and works of Ireland's most distinguished painter of modern times, Jack B Yeats.

Top: the Baroque Room

NUMBER TWENTY NINE

So many of Dublin's 18th-century houses have been pressed into use as offices that it is a pleasure to see this rare example furnished in elegant period style.

The setting Merrion Square epitomises the graciousness of Georgian Dublin. Three of its four sides are enclosed by four-storey redbrick houses, each elegant doorway crowned by a handsome fanlight. The view from the south side towards St Stephen's (also known as the Pepper Canister Church because of the shape of its cupola) is one of the city's most attractive streetscapes, and on the southeast corner of the square stands Number Twenty Nine, the only structure in Dublin to preserve the graceful middle-class domesticity of the 18th century.

Nostalgia You enter, as servants did, through the basement, passing the kitchen and pantry (which has its ingenious rat-proof shelving) to reach the main living quarters on the ground level and parlour floor. Here you will find tasteful Georgian furniture and furnishings, paintings and costumes of the period 1780–1820. The small details are especially captivating – the hastener (tea trolley) in the kitchen, the feather shaving brush in the gentleman's washing room and the exercise machine in the bedroom. Climb to the top floor to see the childrens' playroom with its collection of toys, and on the way up admire the wood carving of Napoleon by Bozzanigo Torino in the master bedroom. Don't miss the exquisite Waterford crystal chandelier and the the fine Mount Mellick embroidery.

HIGHLIGHTS

- Wood carving of Napoleon
- Examples of Mount Mellick embroidery
- Playroom
- Waterford crystal chandelier

INFORMATION

- L10
- 29 Lower Fitzwilliam Street
- 702 6165
- Tue–Sat 10–5; Sun 2–5. Closed two weeks before Christmas
- Café
- Pearse
- 6, 7, 8, 10, 45
- None
- Moderate
- Natural History Museum (➤ 45), National Gallery (➤ 46)
- Visit by guided tour only

Top & right: the Georgian era recaptured inside Number Twenty Nine

25

THE CASINO AT MARINO

HIGHLIGHTS

- Geometrical design
- Corner lions
- Curving wooden doors
- Stucco work
- Marquetry floors

INFORMATION

- ✚ N5
- ✉ Malahide Road
- ☎ 833 1618
- 🕐 Feb, Mar, Nov: Sun, Thu noon–4. Apr: Sun, Thu noon–5. May: daily 10–5. Jun–Sep: daily 10–6. Oct: daily 10–5. (Last admission 45 mins before closing)
- 🚉 Clontarf Road
- 🚌 20A, 20B, 27, 27A, 42, 42C, 123
- ♿ None
- 🍴 Moderate
- ❓ Visit by guided tour only

Exotic woods in a marquetry floor

Once described as 'a flawless and perfectly cut diamond set into the emerald diadem that is Ireland', the Casino has to be the country's most compact and ingenious 18th-century architectural creation.

Inspiration The Casino is now surrounded by modern suburbia. But when viewed in its original rural setting, this deceptively small building must have resembled a Roman temple in Elysian fields. Its enlightened patron was James Caulfield, fourth Viscount Charlemont (1728–99), whose travels in the Mediterranean inspired him to re-create classical elegance and ingenuity in his homeland. To achieve his aims, he enticed King George III's architect, Sir William Chambers (1723–96), to design three buildings on his lands. Of the two that survive, the first is his town house, now home to the Hugh Lane Gallery (► 35), and the second is this delightful little house whose name derives from the Italian word *casa*. Chambers obliged, but curiously, never came to Ireland to see his masterpiece.

Geometry Its floor plan is a Greek cross encircled by pillars on a raised podium with benign lions at each corner creating a diagonal axis. Columns are water pipes, urns are chimneys. What seems from the outside like a single interior space comprises 16 rooms. The four state rooms on the ground floor are perfect in detail – with curving wooden doors, stucco friezes illustrating musical instruments and agricultural implements, and marquetry floors carefully assembled with a variety of rare woods. The whole was 'carefully worked out to produce a totally homogeneous design full of both excitement and repose'.

DUBLIN's
best

MUSEUMS & GALLERIES

Art in Temple Bar

This upbeat part of the city, has two excellent venues showing contemporary work by young artists.

Arthouse Multimedia Centre

➕ K9 ✉ Curved Street
☎ 605 6800 🕐 Mon–Fri 10–5 🚃 Tara Street
🚌 Cross-city buses

Meeting House Square Once night falls, the square's big screen comes alive with an often-changing selection of artists' work. Additionally, the space is used to display 3-D scupltures.

➕ K9 ✉ Temple Bar
🚃 Tara Street
🚌 Cross-city buses

Where coopers made barrels – The Guiness Storehouse

DOUGLAS HYDE GALLERY

Contemporary gallery providing a forum for talent from Ireland and overseas.

➕ K9 ✉ Trinity College, Nassau Street entrance ☎ 608 1116
🕐 Mon–Fri 11–6; Thu 11–7; Sat 11–4:45 🍴 Buttery Bar on campus
🚃 Pearse 🚌 Cross-city buses ♿ Few 🆓 Free

FRY MODEL RAILWAY MUSEUM (► 20)

GALLERY OF PHOTOGRAPHY (► 75)

THE GUINNESS STOREHOUSE

Replacing the Guiness Hop Store and Museum, the Storehouse offers the complete Guiness experience – interactive multimedia exhibition, historical archives, conference facilities, a shop and a free pint of Guiness for each visitor. Sup your pint in the rooftop bar with one of the best views of Dublin.

➕ H9 ✉ St James Gate ☎ 453 6700 🕐 Apr–Sep: daily 9:30–7
(last admission). Oct–Mar: daily 9:30–5 (last admission) 🍴 Bar food
menu 🚌 68A, 78A, 123 and cross-city buses ♿ Good 🆓 Expensive

IRISH JEWISH MUSEUM

The synagogue that opened here in 1918 is now a museum dedicated to the history of Ireland's Jewish community since the mid-19th century.

➕ J10 ✉ 4 Walworth Road, off Victoria Street ☎ 676 0737
🕒 Oct–Apr: Sun only 10:30–2:30. May–Sep: Tue, Thu, Sun 11–3:30
🚌 19, 19A, 22, 22A ♿ Few 💷 Free

NATIONAL WAX MUSEUM

Brings to life everyone from Irish historical figures to the cult cartoon family the Simpsons. You'll find the obligatory Hall of the Megastars and Chamber of Horrors as well as a World of Fairytale and Fantasy.

➕ K7 ✉ Granby Row, Parnell Square ☎ 872 6340 🕒 Mon–Sat 10–5:30; Sun noon–5:30
🍴 Coffee shop 🚌 11, 13, 16, 22, 22A ♿ Few 💷 Moderate

Trophy of musical instruments (1725) in the organ case at St Michan's Church – near the Old Jameson Distillery

OLD JAMESON DISTILLERY

Explore the history of Irish whiskey-making through exhibits and audiovisual presentations on the site of the old Jameson Distillery. Sample a drop of the *uisce beatha*, literally 'water of life', at the visitor bar, which is included in the admission price. Guided tours only.

➕ J8 ✉ Bow Street, Smithfield ☎ 807 2355 🕒 Daily 9–5:15.
Tours every 40 minutes 🍴 Visitor bar 🚌 67, 67A, 68, 69, 79, 90
♿ Good 💷 Moderate

PEARSE MUSEUM

Former school run by Patrick Pearse, the Dublin-born poet and revolutionary executed in 1916 at Kilmainham Gaol (➤ 24).

➕ H16 ✉ St Edna's Park, Grange Road, Rathfarnham ☎ 493 4208
🕒 Nov–Jan: daily 2–4. Feb–Apr, Sep, Oct: daily 2–5. May–Aug: daily 2–5:30 🚌 16 🍴 Tea rooms ♿ Ground floor only 💷 Free

RHA GALLAGHER GALLERY

Prestigious gallery with well-chosen exhibits by Irish and overseas artists. The annual late spring exhibition showcases the best in contemporary Irish art. There is also an attractive outdoor sculpture courtyard.

➕ L10 ✉ 15 Ely Place ☎ 661 2558 🕒 Tue–Sat 11–5; Thu 11–8; Sun 2–5 🚌 Cross-city buses ♿ Good 💷 Free, except for annual exhibition

SHAW BIRTHPLACE

Full of Victorian charm and nostalgia, the childhood home of the playwright George Bernard Shaw (1856–1950) has been restored with great attention to detail.

➕ K10 ✉ 33 Synge Street ☎ 475 0854 or 872 2077
🕒 May–Oct: Mon–Sat 10–5; Sun and public hols 11–5. Closed for tours 1–2 🚌 16, 19, 22 ♿ Few 💷 Moderate

Waterworld

Known to locals as 'the box in the docks', the white cube in the middle of the Grand Canal basin houses the Waterways Visitors Centre. With the help of working and scale models, it traces the story of Ireland's inland waterways and their use for commerce and recreation.

➕ M9 ✉ Grand Canal Quay
☎ 677 7510 🕒 Jun–Sep: daily 9:30–6:30. Oct–May: Wed–Sun 12:30–5
🚆 Lansdowne Road 🚌 3

GEORGIAN DUBLIN

Fitzwilliam Square is lined with red-brick Georgian houses famed for their arched doorways

See Top 25 Sights for
BANK OF IRELAND (► 38)
THE CASINO AT MARINO (► 48)
GENERAL POST OFFICE (► 37)
MARSH'S LIBRARY (► 31)
NEWMAN HOUSE (► 40)
NUMBER TWENTY NINE (► 47)

History

The architectural style of Dublin's magnificent Georgian buildings developed during the reign of kings George I–IV, who occupied the English throne from 1714 to 1830. During this period, the city was planned and laid out with wide boulevards, spacious squares and terraces of elegant town houses. Notable architects were James Gandon, Edward Lovett Pearce, Francis Johnston, Richard Cassels, Robert Parke, Thomas Cooley and William Chambers. Most public buildings are still in use, although visitor access may be restricted.

CUSTOM HOUSE
Designed by James Gandon in 1791, the Custom House (► 16) is an outstanding example of Georgian architecture. The visitor centre has a museum with displays on Gandon's work and the building's history.
➕ L8   ✉ Custom House Quay   ☎ 878 7660   🕐 Mid-Mar to Nov: Mon–Fri 10–5; Sat–Sun 2–5. Nov to mid-Mar: Wed–Fri 10–5; Sun 2–5
🚊 Tara Street   🚌 Cross-city buses   ♿ Very good   💷 Inexpensive

FITZWILLIAM SQUARE
Surrounded by tall elegant buildings, this is one of Dublin's most famous Georgian squares, now given over mostly to offices and apartments. Residents have keys to the gardens.
➕ L10   🚌 10 and cross-city buses   💷 Free

FOUR COURTS
Home to the Irish law courts since 1796, the Four Courts (► 16) has much in common with the Custom House – primarily its designer, James Gandon. The building also suffered fire damage (as did the Custom House) during the turbulent events of 1921. You can visit only when courts are in session.
➕ J9   ✉ Inns Quay   ☎ 872 5555   🚌 Cross-city buses   ♿ Few
💷 Free

GANDON'S RIVER BUILDINGS (► 16)

KING'S INNS

The honourable society of the King's Inns is the impressive setting for Dublin law students training for the bar. Steeped in tradition, this beautiful building was begun by James Gandon. Tours by prior arrangement.

✚ J8 ✉ Henrietta Street ☎ 874 4840 🚍 25, 25A, 66, 67, 90 ♿ Few 💶 Free

LEINSTER HOUSE

Leinster House is the seat of Irish government and home to Dáil Éireann (House of Representatives) and Senead Éireann (Senate). You can visit by prior arrangement when parliament is not in session.

✚ L9 ✉ Kildare Street ☎ 618 3000 🚉 Pearse 🚍 Cross-city buses ♿ Good 💶 Free

MANSION HOUSE

The official residence of the Lord Mayor of Dublin since 1715. In 1919, the first parliament of the Irish people met here to adopt Ireland's Declaration of Independence from Britain. Closed to visitors.

✚ K9 ✉ Dawson Street 🚉 Pearse 🚍 Cross-city buses

MERRION SQUARE

The best preserved Georgian square in Dublin and, as the wall plaques testify, home to many historical Irish figures including Daniel O'Connell and William Butler Yeats. The public park is a hidden gem, well worth exploring after a visit to Number Twenty Nine (► 47).

✚ L9 🚉 Pearse 🚍 5, 7, 7A, 7X, 8, 45 💶 Free

ROYAL COLLEGE OF SURGEONS

One of Dublin's later Georgian constructions, this jewel of a building on the northwest corner of St Stephen's Green, dates from 1806 and was designed by architect Edward Parke. Contact Terry Slattery, Head Porter, in advance to arrange a personal tour.

✚ K9 ✉ St Stephen's Green ☎ 402 2263 🚍 Cross-city buses ♿ Few 💶 Free

TAILOR'S HALL

The Tailor's Hall, dating from 1705, is the only surviving guild hall in Dublin. Inside, the ceiling plasterwork and upper gallery have been painstakingly restored by *An Taisce*, Ireland's National Trust.

✚ J9 ✉ Back Lane, off Christchurch Lane ☎ 454 4794 🚍 Cross-city buses 🕙 By appointment ♿ Few 💶 Free

Georgian houses

Dublin's Georgian houses were built to a basic harmonious design. They generally have five storeys and, typically, pillars and wrought-iron railings, panelled front doors, fanlights and side windows, all combining to create an external symmetry. Inside, the spacious, high-ceilinged rooms are often embellished with elegant stucco work, wood panelling and marble fireplaces.

An elegant Georgian doorway in Fitzwilliam Square with typical gossamer fanlight above

GARDENS & PARKS

Private gardens

Helen Dillon, journalist, lecturer and television presenter, is one of Ireland's best known gardening experts and her own garden reveals how she has put her techniques into practice.

➕ L12 ✉ 45 Sandford Road
🕐 Mar, Jul, Aug: daily 2–6.
Apr–Jun, Sep: Sun 2–6 (by prior arrangement) 🚌 11, 11A, 11B, 44, 44B 🎫 Moderate

Other private gardens open to visitors are listed in an illustrated book, *The Hidden Gardens of Ireland*, published by Gill and Macmillan and available from high street bookshops.

Ducks on the pond expect to be fed by the Dubliners who come in their droves to relax in the peaceful city-centre surroundings of St Stephen's Green

IVEAGH GARDENS

One of Dublin's finest yet least well-known parks. Designed in 1863, these secluded gardens shelter a rustic grotto, cascade fountains, maze, archery grounds, wilderness and woodlands.

➕ K10 ✉ Clonmel Street ☎ 475 7816 🚌 Cross-city buses
🎫 Free

PHOENIX PARK

A vast expanse of green space, lakes and woodland in the heart of the city, this is the largest urban park in Europe, covering some 700ha and encircled by a 13-km wall. Within its confines are Dublin Zoo (▶ 55), the American Ambassador's home and the Irish President's residence, *Áras an Uachtaráin*. The visitor centre is on the site of the old Papal Nunciature, near the Phoenix Monument. The main entrance on Parkgate Street.

➕ From G8 🚌 37 (Castleknock Gate), 10 (Park Gate), 25, 25A, 26, 51, 51B, 66, 66A, 67, 67A (Parkgate Street entrance) 🎫 Free

ST STEPHEN'S GREEN

A hugely popular place when the sun comes out, this park in the centre of the city was originally a piece of common land used for public hangings, among other activities. By 1880, it had become a public garden, thanks to the benevolence of Lord Ardilaun, a member of the Guinness family. Listen for lunchtime concerts and gigs on the bandstand in summer.

➕ K9 🚉 Pearse 🚌 Cross-city buses 🎫 Free

WAR MEMORIAL GARDENS

These wonderful gardens are dedicated to the 49,400 Irish soldiers who died in World War I. Especially moving are the thousands of names etched in the granite book rooms and the beautiful sunken rose gardens. Rowers can sometimes be seen gliding along the River Liffey. Well off the tourist beat.

➕ F9 ✉ Islandbridge ☎ 677 0236 🚌 51, 61 🎫 Free

CHILDREN'S ACTIVITIES

DUBLIN ZOO

More than 700 animals from around the globe live in 24ha of landscaped grounds among the ornamental lakes of Dublin Zoo, many with plenty of room to roam. Visit Monkey Island, the Arctic Fringes and the World of the Primates, and don't miss the Pet Care Area, Reptile House and Discovery Centre. Check out the newborn babies and feeding programmes.

➕ F7 ✉ Phoenix Park ☎ 677 1425 ⏰ Mar–Sep: Mon–Sat 9:30–6; Sun 10:30–6. Oct–Feb: 9:30–4; Sun 10:30–4 Feeding times 11–3:45 🚌 10, 25, 26 🍴 Restaurant, cafés ♿ Good 💷 Expensive

Children's favourite at Dublin Zoo

LAMBERT PUPPET THEATRE

A charming family-run puppet theatre that opened in 1972. The museum upstairs displays a fascinating array of marionettes from around the world. Plays for adults and children include works by W B Yeats and Oscar Wilde. Superlative.

➕ T16 ✉ Clifton Lane, Monkstown ☎ 280 0974 ⏰ Daily 9:30–5 🚆 Salthill and Monkstown 🚌 7, 7A, 8 ♿ Ground floor: good; museum: none 💷 Expensive ❓ Shop

PARNELL CENTRE (▶ 79)

THE ARK

This specially created cultural centre for children offers around ten programmes throughout the year with emphasis on art and culture for children aged 4–14 years.

➕ K9 ✉ Eustace Street ☎ 670 7788 🚆 Tara Street 🚌 Cross-city buses ♿ Good 💷 Depends on activity

VIKING SPLASH TOURS

A most ingenious new tour where passengers are driven through Viking Dublin on amphibious buses before driving into the Grand Canal to finish the tour on water. Fun, educational and exciting.

➕ J9 ✉ Bull Alley Street ☎ 296 6047 ⏰ Tours every half hour Mon–Sat 9–6:30; Sun 11–6:30 💷 Expensive

Feeding children in Dublin

Two excellent child-friendly restaurants that are worth checking out are: Milano, an upmarket, colourful and popular pizza place with patient staff, proving a popular haunt with parents ➕ K9 ✉ Dawson Street ☎ 670 7744 🚆 Pearse 🚌 Cross-city buses and TGI Fridays, a new arrival on the Dublin restaurant scene that understands kids ➕ K9 ✉ St Stephen's Green ☎ 670 7744 🚆 Pearse 🚌 Cross-city buses.

DUBLIN FROM THE DART

Dublin's overground light railway brings you speedily to and from the city

The DART

Dublin Area Rapid Transit is Dublin's light train system, running from the village of Howth, in the north, to Bray in the south. The line follows a coastal route for the most part, with some of the finest views of Dublin. Trains run every five minutes at rush hour, every 20 minutes at off-peak times. Pick up a timetable at any DART station. Try to secure a seat on the side of the train looking out to sea.

BLACKROCK (➤ 70)

BRAY

In the early days of the Kingstown (Dun Laoghaire) Railway, Bray was a sophisticated seaside resort, known as the 'Brighton of Ireland' after England's famous south coast community. Nowadays, this attractive seaside town, at the southern end of the DART line, has become a playground for the young at heart who come for the amusements, dodgem cars and fortune tellers operating on the promenade most of the year round. South County Dubliners come for the fine walks and splendid views around nearby Bray Head.

DUN LAOGHAIRE

Invigorating walks along the piers at Dun Laoghaire, a Victorian seaside resort once known as Kingstown, are something of a Dublin institution. The scenery is stunning, and you can see the ferries plying to and fro across the Irish Sea. The East Pier has a bandstand, folk dancers, rollerbladers and a busy stream of pedestrians. The longer West Pier on the other side is slightly rugged and attracts fishing enthusiasts. Walkers in search of cosy hot toddies and chowder by an open fire will head for the Purty Kitchen pub nearby.

HOWTH

This promontory to the north of Dublin is a traditional fishing village and trendy suburb in one. A popular sailing centre, the Howth marina is always packed with yachts from Ireland and abroad. Howth DART station is near the harbour and close to all the waterside activity, bars and restaurants. Howth is idyllic in sunny weather. It is very busy over the Easter holiday when the place buzzes during one of Ireland's major jazz festivals with bands from all over the world performing in the hotels and pubs throughout the town.

KILLINEY

National and international celebrities such as Bono, Damon Hill, Neil Jordan and Eddie Irvine have settled in the resort known affectionately as Dublin's Riviera. Killiney's distinctly Mediterranean feel is reflected in the names of the magnificent houses, such as La Scala, San Elmo and Mount Etna. Take a walk along the Vico Road for what is arguably the most breathtaking view in Dublin. Look out to Dalkey Island, a craggy piece of land captured by the Vikings and later the site of Christian communities. Fishermen in nearby Coliemore Harbour run boat trips in summer to view the resident goats, ruined oratory and Martello Tower.

SANDYCOVE

James Joyce chose the Martello Tower along the sea front as the setting for the first chapter of *Ulysses* and the museum inside (☎ 280 9265) displays some of his letters, books, photographs and personal possessions. A bracing swim may introduce you to other die-hards who take the plunge all year around. Once gentlemen-only (and nudist to boot!), it is now used by swimmers of both sexes – with suits. Although the DART seems to veer away from the shore at Sydney Parade, it's just a five-minute walk to Sandymount Strand, popular with joggers and dog owners looking for exercise in the morning. After work, Dubliners come here to chill out, stroll, chat and rollerblade. There are good views across to Howth and the north side of Dublin.

Some views from the DART

- Dalkey Island off Killiney
- Sailboats off Dun Laoghaire
- Blackrock's public park and private gardens
- Wetlands bird sanctuary at Booterstown
- Custom House between Tara Street and Connolly Station
- Urban jungle of Kilbarrack, backdrop for novels *The Commitments*, *The Snapper* and *The Van*, Roddy Doyle's prize-winning trilogy.

Howth village and harbour

TRADITIONAL IRISH ENTERTAINMENT

O'Donoghue's singing pub in Merrion Row (see panel below)

Music

Hotel bars are ideal for a quiet drink but it would be a shame to miss the entertainment elsewhere. Dublin pubs are generally busy all week and many host traditional music sessions each evening.

Darkey Kelly's ✚ K9
✉ Cooper Alley, Fishamble Street

O'Donoghue's ✚ L10
✉ Merrion Row

Oliver St John Gogarty ✚ K9
✉ Fleet Street

BURLINGTON CABARET
Nightly cabaret from May to October. Acknowledged rival to Jurys Hotel (► below).
✚ L11 ✉ Burlington Hotel, Upper Leeson Street ☎ 660 5222 🚌 11, 11A, 11B, 13, 46A

INTERNATIONAL BAR
Indulge in a hefty helping of Irish wit at the home of the Comedy Cellar, founded by comic geniuses Ardal O'Hanlon, Dylan Moran and others. The daily evening programme of events emcompasses blues and country music as well as the comedy mainstay.
✚ K9 ✉ 23 Wicklow Street ☎ 677 9250 🚉 Pearse 🚌 Cross-city buses

JURYS CABARET
A hugely popular venue for comedy, music, song and dance from May to October. Book ahead for the show, with or without dinner.
✚ M10 ✉ Jurys Hotel, Ballsbridge ☎ 660 5000 🚉 Lansdowne Road 🚌 5,7, 7A, 7X, 8, 45, 46, 63, 84

O'SHEA'S MERCHANT
Nightly traditional music and dancing – everyone is encouraged to take to the dance floor.
✚ J9 ✉ 12 Lower Bridge Street ☎ 679 6793 🚌 21, 21A

SLATTERY'S
Club kids and octogenarians happily rub shoulders in this traditional pub. A healthy local trade supplies a generous slice of old Dublin, giving way to a younger crowd at weekends.
✚ N10 ✉ Shelbourne Road 🚉 Lansdowne Road 🚌 3, 6, 7, 7A, 7X, 45, 84

VIKING BANQUET
Hearty food accompanied by drama, dance and music. Staff wear traditional costume, and you eat Viking-style from reproduction tableware.
✚ K9 ✉ Viking Adventure, Essex Street, Temple Bar ☎ 490 6077 🚉 Tara Street 🚌 Cross-city buses

ROCK HERITAGE

BAD ASS CAFÉ

Long-established pizza restaurant that once employed a young Sinead O'Connor as a waitress.

⊞ K9 ✉ 9 Crown Alley, Temple Bar
☎ 671 2596 🚉 Tara Street
🚌 Cross-city buses

BAGGOT INN

Moving Hearts put fire in the souls of all those lucky enough to have caught their live performances here. The group had several incarnations over the years – members included Christy Moore, Donal Lunny, Davy Spillane and Declan Sinnott.

⊞ L10 ✉ Lower Baggot Street
☎ 676 1430 🚌 10

U2 – Dublin's most famous band

CAPTAIN AMERICA'S COOKHOUSE

Singer-songwriter Chris De Burgh, of *Lady in Red* fame, got his first live break in this uninspiring burger restaurant.

⊞ K9 ✉ 44 Grafton Street ☎ 671 5266 🚉 Pearse
🚌 Cross-city buses

GRESHAM HOTEL

Once Dublin's grandest hotel, steeped in history. In the 1960s, the Beatles played an impromptu session here, the band's only live performance in Ireland. The forming of the Chieftains, Ireland's greatest exponents of traditional music, also happened here in the 1960s.

⊞ K8 ✉ O'Connell Street ☎ 874 6881 🚌 Cross-city buses

KORKY'S SHOE SHOP

A young Ronan Keating fitted and sold fashionable shoes to trendy youngsters here before hitting the top of the charts with Boyzone.

⊞ K9 ✉ Grafton Street ☎ 670 7943 🚉 Pearse
🚌 Cross-city buses

WINDMILL LANE STUDIOS

Fans still make pilgrimages to the recording and editing studios that nurtured U2 in the early days, before 1987, when their album The Joshua Tree brought them worldwide fame. Small groups gather wistfully outside and leave graffiti messages on the walls as a tribute to their heroes.

⊞ M9 ✉ 4 Windmill Lane, Sir John Rogerson's Quay 🚌 1, 3

Stars

Artists such as Phil Lynott, Rory Gallagher and The Dubliners put Dublin on the musical map and their success was followed in the 1970s and 1980s by The Virgin Prunes and The Boomtown Rats. The following decade saw the emergence of Sinead O'Connor, the Hothouse Flowers and Boyzone. Occupying centre stage is Dublin's greatest musical export – U2, formed in 1978.

Check out the city's musical landmarks with the help of the booklet *Rock 'n Stroll – Dublin's Music Trail*, available from Dublin Tourism and many bookshops.

59

STATUES & MONUMENTS

Jakki McKenna's statue Meeting Place *is better known as 'The Hags with the Bags'*

Nicknames

Political correctness is cast aside in Dublin-speak when referring to the city's sculptures. The Anna Livia fountain on O'Connell Street, symbolising the River Liffey, is known by all as the 'Floozie in the Jacuzzi'. Locals have dubbed the statue of Molly Malone as the 'Tart with the Cart'. Meanwhile, the Dublin shoppers at the north end of the Ha'penny Bridge (see picture above) are the 'Hags with the Bags'.

BRASS FOOTPRINTS

Three sets of brass footprints in the sidewalk run from Westmoreland Street to O'Connell Bridge. This quirky urban art is from the young multi-media artist, Rachel Joynt.
➕ K8 ✉ O'Connell Bridge 🚊 Tara Street 🚌 Cross-city buses

CHILDREN OF LÍR

A poignant Irish fairytale, about three children turned into swans by a wicked stepmother, inspired Oisín Kelly's bronze sculpture (1971). It is the focal point of this garden, dedicated to those who died in pursuit of Irish independence.
➕ K7 ✉ Garden of Remembrance, Parnell Square East ☎ 874 3074 🚌 Cross-city buses

FAMINE FIGURES

A series of emaciated figures along the quays commemorates the Great Famine of 1845–9. Plaques bearing the names of families who suffered will be added over time. (The sculptor Rowan Gillespie is also behind the Spiderman character scaling the Treasury Building on Grand Canal Street.)
➕ L8 ✉ Custom House Quay 🚌 25, 25A, 26, 51, 51B, 66, 66A, 67, 67A

FUSILIERS' ARCH

Also known as Traitors' Arch, this piece on the north-west corner of St Stephen's Green is a tribute to the members of the Royal Dublin Fusiliers killed during the Boer War.
➕ K9/K10 ✉ St Stephen's Green 🚊 Pearse 🚌 Cross-city buses

MOLLY MALONE

The fishmonger of song is believed to have lived in Dublin until her death in 1734.
➕ K9 ✉ Lower Grafton Street 🚊 Pearse 🚌 Cross-city buses

OSCAR WILDE

This languid life-size figure of the famous writer, reclining on a rock at the northwest corner of Merrion Square, is especially haunting at night.
➕ L9 ✉ Merrion Square 🚊 Pearse 🚌 5, 7, 7A, 7X, 8, 45, 46, 84

PATRICK KAVANAGH

Sit and watch the swans slip by with the bronze of poet Patrick Kavanagh (1905–67), who loved this piece of leafy calm in the heart of commercial Dublin.
➕ L10 ✉ Grand Canal, near Baggot Street Bridge 🚌 10

DUBLIN
where to...

ELEGANT DINING

Prices

Approximate prices for a two-course meal for one person with one drink:

£   under IR£15

££   IR£15–IR£35

£££   above IR£35

Things to know

Eating out is extremely popular in Dublin, so book ahead. Many restaurants have terraces; these are open in fine weather. Some restaurants close on Monday. Most serious restaurants offer a fixed-price lunch menu that represents excellent value.

A service charge of 12.5 per cent is generally added and many diners add a tip of about 5 to 10 per cent of the bill. If service is not included, a tip of 12.5–15 per cent is usual.

The restaurants are open for lunch and dinner seven days a week unless otherwise indicated.

THE COMMONS (£££)

A spacious dining room, decorated in Georgian style, on the lower ground floor of Newman House (➤ 40). The menu showcases creative combinations of the finest Irish produce. Stunning terrace.

➕ K9   ✉ 85 St Stephen's Green   ☎ 475 2597   🕐 Lunch, dinner Mon–Fri   🚌 Cross-city buses

COOKE'S CAFÉ (£££)

When it opened in 1992, Cooke's broke new ground in terms of decor and cuisine. The menu, which has strong Californian and Italian influences, includes Caesar salad, angel hair pasta and delicious pecan pie.

➕ K9   ✉ 14 South William Street   ☎ 679 0536   🚌 Pearse   🚌 Cross-city buses

LE COQ HARDI (£££)

Politicians and captains of industry appreciate the genteel formality and discreet service in charmingly appointed rooms. An impressive wine cellar complements the excellent food.

➕ M10   ✉ 35 Pembroke Road, Ballsbridge   ☎ 668 9070   🕐 Lunch Mon–Fri, dinner Mon–Sat   🚌 Lansdowne Road   🚌 5, 7, 7A, 7X, 8, 10, 18, 45, 46, 84

L'ECRIVAIN (£££)

With the recent refurbishment, chef Derry Clarke's popular Irish modern restaurant continues to grow in stature. Friendly service.

➕ L10   ✉ 109a Lower Baggot Street   ☎ 661 1919   🕐 Lunch Mon–Fri, dinner Mon–Sat   🚌 10

ERNIE'S (£££)

An excellent family-run restaurant, filled with the spirit and art of the late Ernie Evans. French cuisine and well-chosen wines.

➕ M12   ✉ Mulberry Gardens, Donnybrook   ☎ 269 3300   🕐 Lunch Tue–Fri, dinner Tue–Sat   🚌 10, 46A, 46B

LES FRERES JACQUES (£££)

Excellent French cooking in a stylish but informal setting. The friendly owner and staff are happy to offer advice on the exquisite menu and wines. Centrally located.

➕ K9   ✉ 74 Dame Street   ☎ 679 4555   🕐 Lunch Mon–Fri, dinner Mon–Sat   🚌 Cross-city buses

PEACOCK ALLEY (£££)

Eclectic cuisine created by trend-setting wunderkind Conrad Gallagher, using the best ingredients in exciting new combinations.

➕ K9/K10   ✉ Fitzwilliam Hotel, St Stephen's Green West   ☎ 478 7015   🕐 Lunch, dinner Mon–Sat   🚌 Pearse   🚌 Cross-city buses

RESTAURANT PATRICK GUILBAUD (£££)

Superlative cuisine by French chef Patrick Guilbaud. Tastefully decorated, with a wonderful collection of Irish art.

➕ L10   ✉ Merrion Hotel, 21 Upper Merrion Street   ☎ 676 4192   🕐 Lunch, dinner Tue–Sat   🚌 Pearse   🚌 5, 7, 7A, 7X, 8, 10, 18, 45, 46

VERY FASHIONABLE

BANG CAFÉ (££)

Cool and minimal, Bang is as trendy and fresh as its get-ahead clientele. The eclectic, modern menu is as fashionable as its cosmopolitan interiors.

✚ L10 ✉ Merrion Row ☎ 675 0898 🚇 Pearse 🚌 5, 7, 7A, 7X, 8, 10, 18, 45, 46

BRASSERIE NA MARA (£££)

A sophisticated, deceptively grand restaurant, frequented by well-heeled locals and the expense account set. The emphasis is on fresh, local seafood. Attentive service.

✚ U15 ✉ The Harbour, Dun Laoghaire ☎ 280 6767 🕐 Lunch Mon–Fri, dinner Mon–Sat 🚇 Dun Laoghaire 🚌 7, 7A, 8

BRUNO'S (££)

A splendid fusion of Irish favourites with French and Mediterranean flavours attracts a hip clientele. Modern and airy, with an affable staff.

✚ K9 ✉ Eustace Street, Temple Bar ☎ 670 6767 🕐 Lunch Mon–Fri, dinner Mon–Sat 🚇 Tara Street 🚌 Cross-city buses

FITZERS (££)

The most fashionable branch of the popular chain. Busy, fiery Mediterranean menu plus chunky burgers and chips.

✚ K9 ✉ 51 Dawson Street ☎ 677 1155 🚇 Pearse 🚌 Cross-city buses

MAO (££)

Colourful place with very modern food and Warholesque lithographs. No reservations, but a fast turn over.

✚ K9 ✉ 2–3 Chatham Row ☎ 670 4899 🚇 Pearse 🚌 Cross-city buses 7, 7A, 8, 46A

ROLY'S BISTRO (££)

Traditional brasserie favoured by Dubliners of the old school, who like hearty food in a busy setting. The chef-patron, Roly Saul, has been at the helm of some of the city's best restaurants.

✚ N11 ✉ 7 Ballsbridge Terrace ☎ 668 2611 🚇 Lansdowne Road 🚌 5, 7, 7A, 7X, 8, 45, 46, 84

SIDE DOOR (££)

Modern restaurant in Dublin's most traditional hotel. Colourful menu, from fish and chips to creatively topped pizzas.

✚ L9 ✉ Shelbourne Hotel, St Stephen's Green ☎ 676 6471 🚇 Pearse 🚌 Cross-city buses

THE TEA ROOMS (£££)

Imaginative, delicately designed dishes in this popular hotel restaurant.

✚ K9 ✉ Clarence Hotel, Temple Bar ☎ 670 7766 🕐 Lunch Mon–Fri, dinner Mon–Sat 🚇 Tara Street 🚌 Cross-city buses

VELURE (££)

The place for fashionable thirtysomethings, the plush decor, lurid cocktails and easy listening soundtrack provide for atmospheric dining. Trendy menu combining tasty Eastern, Irish and Mediterranean cuisine.

✚ K9 ✉ 47 South William Street ☎ 670 5585 🕐 Brunch Sun noon–6, dinner Tue–Sat 🚇 Pearse 🚌 Cross-city buses

In vogue

Dublin's reputation as a fashionable youth-oriented city is borne out by the capital's cosmopolitan restaurant scene. Listed on these pages are the city's most popular haunts and you should make reservations as far ahead as possible.

Many of Dublin's trendier restaurants have two evening seatings at weekends. The early seating is usually around 7PM while the later seating is from approximately 9:30PM. If you want to linger, be sure your table is not booked for a second party.

IRISH CUISINE

Celtic cooking

Today's Irish cooking draws inspiration from many sources but simplicity is the key when it comes to serving fresh local produce. Smoked salmon, oysters, hearty soups and stews are readily available in most Dublin restaurants and pubs, sometimes accompanied by soda bread, a dense yeast-free loaf that goes well with traditional dishes. Irish restaurants come in many guises: some adopt a traditional style serving comfort food, such as seafood chowder and Irish stew, in settings with turf fires and local music, while others are culinary trend setters nationally and internationally.

AVOCA (£)

First city centre branch of this quality Irish store with a restaurant that serves some of the tastiest salad and farmhouse around. Wholesome Irish with modern Mediterranean touches.
K9 ✉ Suffolk Street ☎ 873 2687 🕓 Lunch and snacks daily until 5 🚆 Pearse 🚌 Cross-city buses

CONWAYS (££)

A timeless watering-hole, where Dubliners have been coming to sample fine food and drink since 1745. Near the museums.
K8 ✉ 70 Parnell Street ☎ 873 2687 🚌 Cross-city buses

EDEN (£££)

Contemporary restaurant, with predominantly white decor and floor-to-ceiling windows, serving modern Irish food with a Mediterranean slant. Pleasant venue on summer evenings. Also popular for Saturday lunch when the Temple Bar food market is in full swing outside.
K9 ✉ Meeting House Square ☎ 670 5372 🚆 Tara Street 🚌 Cross-city buses

GALLAGHERS BOXTY HOUSE (££)

Traditional food centred on the boxty, an Irish potato pancake. Try the brown bread ice cream.
K9 ✉ 20–1 Temple Bar ☎ 677 2762 🚆 Tara Street 🚌 Cross-city buses

LÍADAIN'S RESTAURANT (££)

Authentic Irish menu, music and atmosphere.
K11 ✉ 17 Ranelagh ☎ 497 8240 🕓 Lunch, dinner Wed–Mon 🚌 11, 11B, 62

MERMAID CAFÉ (£££)

Traditional Irish fare served in a contemporary, minimalist style. Popular with the fashionable set, lured by the purest ingredients and tasty dishes like the New England crab cakes.
K9 ✉ 69–70 Dame Street ☎ 670 8236 🚌 Cross-city buses

PIER 32 (££)

Exciting choices in a casual, nautical setting, emphasising the fish dishes on the broad menu. Everything is super-fresh and authentic.
L10 ✉ 23 Upper Pembroke Street 🕓 Lunch Mon–Fri, dinner Mon–Sat ☎ 676 1494 🚌 10, 13, 46A, 46B

THORNTONS (£££)

Celebrated restaurant owned by chef Kevin Thornton who prepares nothing short of Irish culinary masterpieces.
J11 ✉ 1 Portobello Road ☎ 454 9067 🕓 Lunch Tue–Sat, dinner Tue–Thu, Sat 🚌 16 16A, 16B, 19, 22A, 22B, 47A, 47B, 49

WRENNS (££)

A traditional setting for progressive Irish dishes. The menu changes seasonally to allow for maximum quality and flavour.
M13 ✉ 24–25 Upper Camden Street (above Bleeding Horse Pub) ☎ 478 2101 🚌 19A, 44, 47A, 47B and cross-city buses

INTERNATIONAL CUISINE

INDIAN

EASTERN TANDOORI (££)

Well known for its range of authentic dishes.

⊞ K9 ⊠ 34–35 South William Street ☎ 671 0506 🕐 Lunch Mon–Sat, dinner daily 🚇 Pearse 🚌 Cross-city buses

RAJDOOT TANDOORI (£££)

Dependable North Indian food, excellent service and pleasant surroundings.

⊞ K9 ⊠ Westbury Hotel, Clarendon Street ☎ 679 4274 🕐 Lunch Mon–Sat, dinner daily 🚇 Pearse 🚌 Cross-city buses

ITALIAN

KAPRIOL (£££)

For years Dubliners have been coming to dine casually amid kitsch surroundings and wooden booths for privacy; extensive menu and wine list.

⊞ M13 ⊠ 45 Lower Camden Street ☎ 475 1235 🕐 Dinner only Thu–Sat 🚇 19A, 44, 47A, 47B and cross-city buses

STEPS OF ROME (£)

Divine pizza by the slice plus other gutsy fare.

⊞ K9 ⊠ Chatham Street ☎ 670 5630 🚇 Pearse 🚌 Cross-city buses

TRENTUNO (££)

Bright, modern restaurant with varied menu offering huge portions of favourite Italian dishes.

⊞ K9 ⊠ 31 Wicklow Street ☎ 677 4190 🚇 Pearse 🚌 Cross-city buses

UNICORN (££)

Bustling Italian restaurant where the people-watching is as satisfying as the food. Saturday lunch is an institution.

⊞ L10 ⊠ 12b Merrion Court, off Merrion Road ☎ 676 2182 🕐 Lunch, dinner Mon–Sat 🚇 Pearse 🚌 5, 7, 7A, 7X, 8, 10, 18, 45, 46

THAI

CHILI CLUB (££)

Small Thai restaurant selling tasty food.

⊞ K9 ⊠ 1 Anne's Lane, off South Anne's Street ☎ 677 3721 🕐 Lunch Mon–Sat, dinner daily 🚇 Pearse 🚌 Cross-city buses

OTHER ASIAN FARE

LANGKAWI (££)

Excellent Malaysian restaurant with an exciting, extensive menu. Totally tasty food that's high on flavour.

⊞ M10 ⊠ 46 Upper Baggot Street ☎ 668 2760 🕐 Lunch Mon–Fri, dinner Mon–Sat 🚇 Lansdowne Road 🚌 10, 18

WAGAMAMA (££)

Fast and furious woks churn out healthy substantial Japanese dishes in a minimalist environment.

⊞ K9 ⊠ St Stephen's Green Shopping Centre, South King Street ☎ 662 0233 🚇 Pearse 🚌 Cross-city buses

YAMAMORI NOODLES (££)

Japanese noodle and sushi house frequented by young Dubliners.

⊞ K9 ⊠ 71–2 South Great Georges Street ☎ 475 5001 🚌 Cross-city buses

More exotic flavours

Other restaurants with an international flavour include: **Don Angel** with *tapas* and occasional flamenco music ⊠ 7 d'Olier Street ☎ 679 3859; **Aya** Dublin's hippest sushi bar ⊠ Clarendon Street ☎ 677 1544; **Sinners** with Lebanese delicacies ⊠ 12 Parliament Street ☎ 671 9345; **Marrakesh** with Moroccan fare ⊠ 28 South Anne's Street ☎ 679 4409; **Tante Zoe's** for Creole cooking ⊠ 1a Crow Street Temple Bar ☎ 679 4407

VEGETARIAN FARE & SEAFOOD

A good catch

Fresh fish is plentiful in Dublin restaurants. Oysters, mussels, crab, prawns, salmon, ray, mackerel, sole, whiting and trout are all found in local waters. They work equally well when cooked plainly, to intensify the flavours, or incorporated into more elaborate dishes. For a truly Irish gastronomic experience, wash down a dozen fresh oysters with a glass of Guinness and mop up the salty juices with home-baked brown bread.

Monday is the one day of the week when the choice of fresh fish is limited. In Ireland, fishermen still take a rest on Sunday, so there are no deliveries the following day.

BLAZING SALADS (£)

Interesting salads and vegetarian fare. Popular with shoppers.

✚ K9 ✉ 21c Powerscourt Townhouse Centre, Clarendon Street ☎ 671 9552 🕓 Lunch and snacks until 6 Mon–Sat 🚌 Cross-city buses

CAVISTONS (££)

Immensely popular restaurant that arose from the success of the neighbouring shop. Fashionable fresh food with a Mediterranean slant.

✚ W17 ✉ 59 Glasthule Road, Sandycove ☎ 280 9245 🕓 Lunch until 6 Tue–Sat 🚇 Sandycove & Glasthule 🚌 8

CORNUCOPIA (£)

Long-established city-centre restaurant and shop with optional take-away service.

✚ K9 ✉ 19 Wicklow Street ☎ 677 7583 🕓 Breakfast, lunch and dinner Mon–Sat 🚇 Pearse 🚌 Cross-city buses

GUINEA PIG (THE FISH RESTAURANT (£££)

Family-run restaurant, adorned with rustic brass ornaments and decorative plates, with an extensive, though not exclusively, seafood-based menu.

✚ Off map to southeast ✉ 17 Railway Road, Dalkey ☎ 285 9055 🕓 Dinner only 🚇 Dalkey 🚌 8

JUICE (£)

Vegetarian food and juice bar with a globally inspired menu that includes Japanese, Italian, Mexican and Caribbean dishes.

✚ K9 ✉ 73–83 South Great Georges Street ☎ 475 7856 🚌 Cross-city buses

KING SITRIC (£££)

The fish are landed just a few metres from Dublin's most regal seafood restaurant. Popular with Dublin high society and visting gastronomes. Wonderful menu and wine cellar.

✚ BB10 (inset) ✉ East Pier, Howth ☎ 832 5235 🕓 Lunch Mon–Fri, dinner Mon–Sat 🚇 Howth 🚌 31, 31B

LORD EDWARD (£££)

Dublin's oldest seafood restaurant serves a wide range of fish dishes, from Galway Bay oysters to Sole Véronique in traditional surroundings.

✚ J9 ✉ 22 Christchurch Place ☎ 454 2420 🕓 Lunch Mon–Fri, dinner Mon–Sat 🚌 Cross-city buses

OCEAN (£)

Glass surrounded bar and restaurant with marvellous waterside view. The menu offers delicate portions of fresh shellfish and seafood along with wraps and salads. Perfect for sunny summer lunches.

✚ M9 ✉ Grand Canal Basin ☎ 668 8862 🕓 Lunch, dinner Mon–Sat 🚇 Landsdowne Road 🚌 3

WRIGHTS BRASSERIES (££)

Busy restaurant owned by Dublin's most successful fishmongers. Attractive home-style food.

✚ T16 ✉ The Crescent, Monkstown ☎ 280 5174 🕓 Lunch, dinner Mon–Sat 🚇 Salthill & Monkstown 🚌 7, 7A, 8

PUBS & CASUAL DINING

CAFÉ EN SEINE (£)

Exquisite pastries, carvery lunch and excellent Sunday brunch set in a beautiful interior with strikingly high ceilings. Service can be erratic in the evening.

🔲 K9 ✉ 40 Dawson Street ☎ 677 4369 🚉 Pearse 🚌 Cross-city buses

THE CHOCOLATE BAR (£)

Hot and cold designer sandwiches by day for trendies and office workers; a popular drinking haunt by night. Great cocktails.

🔲 K10 ✉ Old Harcourt Street Station, Upper Hatch Street ☎ 478 0166 🍴 Food served at lunch only 🚌 Cross-city buses

COCOON (£)

Modern, chic and sleek, this hotel-lobby style bar serves champagne and chips in equal quantities to Dublin's smart snackers.

🔲 K9 ✉ Royal Hibernian Way ☎ 679 6259 🍴 Food served at lunch only 🚉 Pearse 🚌 Cross-city buses

DOCKERS (£)

Basic quayside pub frequented by old-style Dubliners as well as actors, film folk and musicians. Made fashionable by the likes of U2 and Jim Sheridan, this is one of the city's best places for sausage sandwiches and pints of Guinness.

🔲 M8 ✉ 5 Sir John Rogerson's Quay ☎ 677 1692 🍴 Food served at lunch only 🚌 1, 3, 53A

EDDIE ROCKETS (£)

US-style diners offering burgers, fries, hot dogs, buffalo wings and shakes with sassy service to anthems from a 1950s jukebox. Open from breakfast until midnight during the week, until the wee hours Thu–Sat. Branches city-wide. Check the telephone directory for your nearest.

FRONT LOUNGE (£)

Excellent lunchtime salads, Mediterranean and Thai dishes.

🔲 K9 ✉ Parliament Street ☎ 679 3988 🍴 Food served at lunch only 🚌 Cross-city buses

THE GLOBE (£)

Delicious home-made soup, sandwiches from Cooke's Café (► 62), and a mouth-watering array of pastries.

🔲 K9 ✉ 11 South Great Georges Street ☎ 671 1220 🚌 Cross-city buses

INKWELL BAR (£)

The bar in this small hotel is like a sitting room, and there are tables outside in summer. You can get tasty sandwiches and hearty specials all day.

🔲 M10 ✉ Schoolhouse Hotel, Northumberland Road ☎ 667 5014 🍴 Food served at lunch only 🚉 Lansdowne Road 🚌 5, 6, 7, 7A, 7X, 8, 45, 46, 84

THOMAS READ (£)

Brasserie with an extensive menu of imaginative, freshly prepared home-style dishes. One of the best pub lunches in Dublin.

🔲 K9 ✉ 4 Parliament Street ☎ 671 7283 🍴 Food served at lunch only 🚌 Cross-city buses

Pub life

Café society is rivalled only by pub life in Dublin. Most streets have at least one bustling 'local' where people spend hours swapping stories and gossip until closing time at 11PM (11:30PM in summer). Irish pubs are independently owned and each has its own character and flavour, which means that Dubliners have very precise feelings about the pub they choose to frequent. Some of the older pubs have cosy snugs where you can retreat for a hot whiskey or port on a cold day.

BREAKFAST, BRUNCH & SNACKS

Early start

The traditional Irish breakfast consists of bacon, sausage, egg, mushrooms, tomato, black and white pudding and toast, washed down with strong tea or coffee. But few working Dubliners have time to indulge, except perhaps at weekends. Led by the power breakfast business community, city dwellers are beginning to eat out first thing in the morning. New places are always opening or extending their menus, so keep an eye open.

ALPHA RESTAURANT (£)

Traditional café that serves all-day breakfast as well as huge mixed grills and snacks. Terrific for the morning after the night before.

K9 ✉ Corner Wicklow Street and Clarendon Street ☎ 677 0213 🕔 Breakfast, lunch and dinner Mon–Sat 🚇 Pearse 🚌 Cross-city buses

CAFÉ IRIE (£)

Laid back, bohemian young café that is especially good for hearty breakfasts. Home-style snacks and big mugs of coffee keep diners going throughout the day.

K9 ✉ 11 Fownes Street, Temple Bar ☎ 672 5090 🕔 Breakfast, lunch and snacks Mon–Sat 🚇 Tara Street 🚌 Cross-city buses

CAFÉ JAVA (££)

Plenty for all tastes and appetites in both branches of this popular breakfast haunt. Frequent queues, but newspapers help pass the time.

L11; K9 ✉ 145 Upper Leeson Street; 5 South Anne's Street ☎ 660 0675; 670 7239 🕔 Breakfast and lunch 🚇 Pearse 🚌 11, 11A, 11B, 13, 46A and cross-city buses

ELEPHANT AND CASTLE (££)

Widest breakfast menu in Dublin with straight-forward American cuisine. Well worth the wait even when queues are long.

K9 ✉ 18 Temple Bar ☎ 679 3121 🕔 Breakfast, lunch and dinner 🚇 Tara Street 🚌 Cross-city buses

EXPRESSO BAR (££)

Matte black and chrome café-restaurant with two centrally located branches. Fashionable food, delicate pastries and herbal teas.

M10 ✉ St Mary's Road ☎ 660 0585 🕔 Breakfast, lunch and dinner 🚇 Lansdowne Road 🚌 5, 7, 7A, 7X, 8, 10, 45,

FITZERS CAFÉ (££)

Trendy chain café with hi-tech decor; great for salads, pasta and Sunday brunch.

K9 ✉ Temple Bar Square ☎ 679 0440 🕔 Breakfast, lunch and dinner 🚇 Tara Street 🚌 Cross-city buses

NUDE (£)

Healthy fast food with an organic slant and the most creative combinations in wraps, salads and smoothies. Stark interiors complement the postmodern packaging and presentation.

K9 ✉ Suffolk Street ☎ 677 4804 🚇 Pearse 🚌 Cross-city buses

ODESSA LOUNGE & GRILL (££)

This 1970s-inspired restaurant attracts a hip clientele. A favourite for late Sunday brunch.

K9 ✉ 13–14 Dame Court ☎ 670 7634 🕔 Brunch and dinner Sat, Sun, dinner Mon–Fri 🚇 Pearse 🚌 Cross-city buses

TÁ SÉ MAHOGANÍ GASPIPES (£££)

Sunday brunch with newspapers and a menu that includes good vegetarian choices.

H8 ✉ 17 Manor Street ☎ 679 8138 🚌 37, 39, 39A, 70, 70X and cross-city buses

COFFEE & AFTERNOON TEA

BEWLEY'S ORIENTAL CAFÉS (£)
Wonderful tea, coffee, pastries, cakes and buns, as well as traditional breakfasts and adequate cold lunches. Central branches stay open late (► side panel).

BT2 (£)
Glass-fronted café in the BT2 store with great views of Grafton Street. Sit in white minimalist splendour nibbling tasty sandwiches, pastries and salads or simply while away the afternoon over frothy coffees, hot chocolate or fresh juices.
✚ K9 ✉ Grafton Street ☎ 679 5666 🕐 Breakfast, lunch and snacks 🚇 Pearse 🚌 Cross-city buses

BUTTERY BRASSERIE (£)
A stylish clientele at which outdoor tables are especially good for long, lazy coffee-drinking and people-watching.
✚ K9 ✉ 2 Royal Hibernian Way, Dawson Street ☎ 679 6259

GLORIA JEANS (£)
Everything for the coffee lover from hi-tech paraphernalia to frothy, double lattes. Wide range of Arabica coffee beans to buy.
✚ K9 ✉ Powerscourt Townhouse Centre, Clarendon Street ☎ 679 7772 🕐 Lunch, coffee and snacks Mon–Sat 🚇 Pearse 🚌 Cross-city buses

KAFFE MOCHA (£)
A coffee house with over 50 types of coffee and an extensive menu of sandwiches, snacks and tasty main dishes. Newspapers, board games; library upstairs.
✚ K9 ✉ 39 South William Street ☎ 679 8475 🕐 Daily 8AM–4AM 🚇 Pearse 🚌 Cross-city buses

METRO CAFÉ (£)
Coffee, tea, hot chocolate and flavoursome light food. Newspapers.
✚ K9 ✉ 43 South William Street ☎ 679 4515 🚇 Pearse 🚌 Cross-city buses

PLANET CYBER CAFÉ (£)
One of the many internet cafés springing up around the city. Coffee, web and email access, plus deli fare.
✚ K9 ✉ 23 South Great Georges Street ☎ 679 0583 🚌 Cross-city buses

SHELBOURNE HOTEL (£)
The Lord Mayor's Lounge is the grandest of Dublin addresses for elegant afternoon tea with its dainty sandwiches, cakes, scones and savoury morsels. Reserve ahead.
✚ L9 ✉ 27 St Stephen's Green North 🕐 Afternoon tea 3PM–5:30PM ☎ 676 6471 🚇 Pearse 🚌 Cross-city buses

WESTBURY HOTEL (£)
Afternoon tea takes place in the large, open foyer, often accompanied by a pianist or fashion show.
✚ K9 ✉ Balfe Street, off Grafton Street 🕐 Afternoon tea. Last orders 7PM ☎ 679 1122 🚇 Pearse 🚌 Cross-city buses

Bewley's
Steeped in local history and folklore, Bewley's Oriental cafés are a Dublin institution. The surroundings in the older premises (Westmoreland Street and Grafton Street) are glorious – old wooden panelled rooms, stained glass, vast coffee canisters and the inward-sloping banquettes which provide the ideal position in which to recline with a newspaper. Bewley's cafés are prime locations for people-watching. Branches are at: 78 Grafton Street; 40 Mary Street; 10–12 Westmoreland Street; Santry and the airport.

SHOPPING DISTRICTS

Tax-free shopping

In Ireland, VAT is charged on most goods at 21 per cent but it can be claimed back if purchases are taken out of the country within three months thanks to the VAT (Value Added Tax) Retails Export Scheme. Ask the shop assistant for VAT vouchers at point of purchase. On departure, the VAT-back desk in the arrivals hall at Dublin or Shannon airport will help you with your claim. You may be asked to to present the goods for inspection, and if the vouchers exceed IR£200, you may need authorisation from the nearby customs desk. Allow about 30 minutes.

BLACKROCK
Bargain hunters flock to Blackrock, 8km south of Dublin, for the market held every Saturday and Sunday, 10–5. Stalls sell clothes, bric-à-brac, crafts and antiques. Easy to reach by bus and the DART (► 56, 91).

FRANCIS STREET
Dublin's antique quarter, close to Christ Church Cathedral, has beautiful furniture, Irish silver, wonderful speciality pieces and *objets d'art*. There are few bargains but the staff in the various shops are helpful and experienced in shipping purchases overseas. The Gallic Kitchen on 49 Francis Street is good for coffee.

GRAFTON STREET
The city's busy pedestrianised main shopping thoroughfare runs south from College Green to St Stephen's Green showcasing Dublin life at its most colourful. On either side are shops, department stores (including Brown Thomas), flower sellers, street musicians, hair braiders and jewellery stalls. Plenty of restaurants, pubs and cafés when you are tired of shopping.

HENRY STREET
A busy pedestrian area, north of the River Liffey, where Irish and international chain stores, sports retailers, discount outlets, musicians and braying street vendors jostle for attention. Teeming with shoppers all day, so come early before things get too chaotic.

JOHNSONS COURT
Exclusive little shopping enclave off Grafton Street packed with some of Dublin's best jewellers and speciality shops. With the old-fashioned shop fronts, narrow walkways and Dickensian street lamps, you may feel you have slipped back in time, at first, but the prices will bring you right up to date.

SOUTH GREAT GEORGES STREET
A bohemian part of town filled with second-hand clothes shops, ethnic shops and fashionable restaurants and bars. Fortune tellers, body piercers and second-hand record stallholders rub shoulders in George's Street Arcade, the starting point. This area is hugely popular with Dublin's students and style gurus in search of a bargain and a touch of individuality.

TEMPLE BAR
Busy Temple Bar (► 75) may have a reputation for being a bit bohemian, but as the area starts to settle into itself, you may well find many interesting ways to spend your money. In addition to all the speciality shops and markets, there are galleries, craft shops, jewellers and souvenir shops. Restaurants and pubs abound, the latter often with live music.

SHOPPING CENTRES & DEPARTMENT STORES

ARNOTTS

This large department store stocks everything from the traditional to the fashionable in clothes, interiors, household, leisure, entertainment and cosmetics.

🔁 K8 ✉ Henry Street
☎ 805 0400 🚉 Tara Street
🚌 Cross-city buses

BROWN THOMAS

Ireland's stylish department store showcases Irish and international designer clothes. Also homeware, cosmetics, leather goods, accessories and linens. A subsidiary, BT2, also in Grafton Street, has a café with terrific views (➤ 69).

🔁 K9 ✉ Grafton Street
☎ 605 6666 🚉 Pearse
🚌 Cross-city buses

CLERY'S

A Dublin institution. Many romantic assignations have been made beneath the clock outside this department store. Refurbishment has brightened it up.

🔁 K8 ✉ O'Connell Street,
☎ 878 6000 🚉 Tara Street
🚌 Cross-city buses

DEBENHAMS

Four floors of cosmetics, accessories, fashion, homeware, lingerie and gift items include the affordable 'Designers at Debenhams' collection.

🔁 K8 ✉ Jervis Street
Shopping Centre, Henry Street
☎ 878 1222 🚉 Pearse
🚌 Cross-city buses

DUNNES STORES

Ireland's Marks and Spencer, is known for good value. Much of the fashion, lingerie, home-ware, hardware, food and leisure items carry the store's own St Bernard label. Branches city-wide.

🔁 K9 ✉ St Stephen's
Green Shopping Centre
☎ 478 0188 🚉 Pearse Street
🚌 Cross-city buses

POWERSCOURT TOWNHOUSE CENTRE

A warren of boutiques, gift and craft shops, restaurants, cafés and art galleries within a converted Georgian townhouse. The Design Centre stocks clothing by more than 20 Irish fashion designers, with everything from power suits to flamboyant evening wear; the antiques gallery upstairs is bursting with Irish and international treasures. A recent make-over of the centre has introduced new vitality.

🔁 K9 ✉ Clarendon Street
🚉 Pearse 🚌 Cross-city buses

ROYAL HIBERNIAN WAY

Select mall with trendy boutiques, jewellers, opticians, speciality food shops and a very cool café/bar.

🔁 K9 ✉ Dawson Street

WESTBURY MALL

Small shops sell soft furnishings, candles, jewellery, accessories, lingerie, flowers and gifts in this mall joining the Westbury Hotel to Johnson's Court, parallel to Grafton Street.

🔁 K9 ✉ Balfe Street, off
Grafton Street 🚉 Pearse
🚌 Cross-city buses

Blanchardstown

This massive mall, about 20 minutes drive from town, has supermarkets, department stores, cinemas and, more importantly, the best selection of price-wise and fashionable local and international retail names under one roof in the Dublin area: Miss Selfridge, Principles, Oasis, Boots, Evans and Warehouse.

🔁 Off map to south
✉ Blanchardstown, County
Dublin 🚉 Blanchardstown
🚌 22B, 39, 70

71

MEN & WOMEN'S CLOTHING

Ireland's international designers

Dublin fashion stores carry a great mix of contemporary, alternative and classic collections. Irish designers to look for include Paul Costelloe, Lainey Keogh, Daryl Kerrigan and Philip Treacy. Check out Orla Keily's handbags, Vivienne Walsh's intricate jewellery, Pauric Sweeney's witty postmodern accessories (stocked at Hobo right) and Slim Barrett's fairytale tiaras.

ALIAS TOM
One of Dublin's longest-standing men's stores. High fashion on the ground floor and a great selection of suits below: Paul Smith, Versace, Issay Miyake, Donna Karan, Calvin Klein, Hugo Boss, and many, many more.
⊞ K9 ✉ Duke Lane ☎ 671 5443 ▣ Pearse ▣ Cross-city buses

AWEAR
Fashionable clothes for young women, with reassuring price tags, this is Ireland's own high street chain store that offers plenty by way of choice. Stock changes every two weeks.
⊞ K9 ✉ Grafton Street and other branches ☎ 671 7200 ▣ Pearse ▣ Cross-city buses

BT2
Brown Thomas' trendy younger sibling sells the sports and diffusion lines by Prada, Dolce e Gabbana and Paul Smith. Wonderful views of Grafton Street.
⊞ K9 ✉ Grafton Street ☎ 605 6666 ▣ Pearse ▣ Cross-city buses

DESIGN CENTRE, POWERSCOURT TOWNHOUSE (➤ 71)

HOBO
Flagship store of Ireland's most credible and successful street-wear shops. Own-label fleeces, sweats, cords and combats for men, women and teenagers.
⊞ K9 ✉ 6–9 Trinity Street ☎ 670 4869 ▣ Cross-city buses

LOUIS COPELAND
Acquiring a Louis Copeland suit, made-to-measure or off the peg, is a rite of passage for well-dressed Irish men. The tailor of choice for politicians and society figures.
⊞ L10 ✉ 30 Lower Pembroke Street ☎ 661 0110 ▣ 10

LOUISE KENNEDY
The understated elegance of Ireland's leading designer appeals to those with taste. The restored Georgian residence is stylish and calm and exudes confidence, just like Kennedy's clothing and crystal collections that are sold alongside luxury branded accessories, gift items and homeware.
⊞ L9 ✉ 56 Merrion Square ☎ 662 0056 ▣ Pearse ▣ 5, 7, 7A, 7X, 8, 10, 45, 46, 84

SUSAN HUNTER
Tiny but exclusive lingerie shop. Ireland's only source of La Perla and Tatebankum. Pricey but irresistible.
⊞ K9 ✉ 13 Westbury Mall ☎ 679 1271 ▣ Pearse ▣ Cross-city buses

TRIBE
A favourite shop for Ireland's urban skaters and surfers, Karl Swan's laid-back store is crammed with well-chosen casual clothes, shoes and accessories.
⊞ K9 ✉ First Floor, St Stephen's Green Centre ☎ 475 0311 ▣ Pearse ▣ Cross-city buses

SECOND-HAND & RETRO CLOTHING

A STORE IS BORN
A garage-style space open on Saturdays only, this is a great source of alternative party wear for men and women, rated highly by those in the know. Worth checking out.

✚ K9 ✉ 34 Clarendon Street ☎ 679 5866 🚉 Pearse 🚌 Cross-city buses

CHARLEY'S AUNT
Owned by Charley Rankin, who used to supply all of Dublin's vintage shops with clothes, jewellery and accessories. His basement shop is retro heaven and a real treasure trove.

✚ K9 ✉ 25 South William Street ☎ 087 235 6349 🚉 Pearse 🚌 Cross-city buses

FLIP
One of the first ports of call for trendy Irish shoppers on the trail of second-hand jeans, checked shirts, baseball jackets, bowling bags and other bits of Americana.

✚ K9 ✉ 4 Upper Fownes Street, Temple Bar ☎ 671 4299 🚉 Tara Street 🚌 Cross-city buses

HARLEQUIN
Upscale vintage clothing and accessories. Especially good for women's coats.

✚ K9 ✉ 13 Castle Market ☎ 671 0202 🚉 Pearse 🚌 Cross-city buses

JENNY VANDER
The place for intricate eveningwear, coats, dresses and separates in delicate and luxurious fabrics as well as shoes, handbags and jewellery from another era. It's all more antique than second-hand.

✚ K9 ✉ 20 Georges Street Arcade, South Great Georges Street ☎ 677 0406 🚌 Cross-city buses

RUFUS THE CAT
The hippest in retro accessories and men's suits from the 1950s to 1970s, plus some fantastic accessories – early digital watches a speciality. In the same building as Jenny Vander.

✚ K9 ✉ 20 Georges Street Arcade, South Great Georges Street ☎ 677 0406 🚌 Cross-city buses

SÉSÍ PROGRESSIVE
Racks of trendy second-hand clothing, all with affordable price tags. A favourite with Dublin's college kids.

✚ K9 ✉ 11 Fownes Street Lower, Temple Bar ☎ 677 4779 🚉 Tara Street 🚌 Cross-city buses

STOCK EXCHANGE
A swap shop where designer labels abound in all shapes, sizes and styles. Stock is gathered from private clients and often from shops and boutiques. Trust to luck.

✚ M10 ✉ 8 Upper Baggot Street ☎ 668 8010 🚌 10

WILD CHILD
Kitsch and quirky retro clothing, cards, buttons, accessories and cosmetics. Everything for anyone impersonating Elvis or the Pink Ladies, immortalised in the hit musical *Grease*.

✚ K9 ✉ 61 and 77 South Great Georges Street ☎ 475 5099 🚌 Cross-city buses

Buried treasure
Although Dubliners tend to be hoarders by nature, the city has always had a great choice of antique, retro and second-hand clothing stores. If you are lucky, you can uncover genuine treasures for just a few pounds in these shops and at market stalls. In fact, some items may have been rented or loaned out to wardrobe departments on film sets, so you could be buying a celebrity castoff.

ANTIQUES & ART

Craftsmanship

Dublin's rich reputation as a centre of creative excellence dates back several centuries. Irish furniture and silver of the Georgian period embodies some of the finest craftmanship of the late 18th and early 19th centuries (the harp in the hallmark indicates a piece was made in Ireland) and early 20th-century Irish art has attracted worldwide acclaim. Antiques fairs take place regularly in Dublin; the most prestigious events are held two to three times a year at the Royal Dublin Society. For news of auctions around the city, check the daily newspapers.

APOLLO GALLERY

Dedicated primarily to the work of Graham Knuttal, whose distinctive form of cubism has attracted recognition from international collectors, restaurant designers and Hollywood stars like Sylvester Stallone.

K9   51c Dawson Street
671 2609   Pearse
Cross-city buses

IB JORGENSEN FINE ART

Ireland's favourite fashion designer turned to fine art in 1992 and hasn't looked back. Prepare to pay top prices for works by Jack Yeats, Walter Frederick Osbourne and Mary Swanzy.

L9   29 Molesworth Street
661 9758   Pearse
Cross-city buses

JOHN FARRINGTON ANTIQUES

This small shop is packed to the gills with Irish furniture, silver, glass and *objets d'art*. The precious antique jewellery is especially coveted. Clients include film stars, rock musicians and super-models.

K9   32 Drury Street
679 1899   Pearse
Cross-city buses

KERLIN GALLERY

Arguably Dublin's leading contemporary gallery, established in 1988, showing the work of top artists like Dorothy Cross, Feilim Egan, David Godbold and Paul Seawright. National and international exhibitions are staged monthly.

K9   Anne's Lane, off South Anne's Street
670 9093   Pearse
Cross-city buses

LEMON STREET GALLERY

As refreshing to the Irish arts scene as the name would suggest, this gallery offers an intimidation free zone to those wishing to look at framed and unframed work by a wide range of Irish and international artists. Monthly exhibitions ensure a steady flow of new work.

K9   Lemon Street, off Grafton Street   671 0244
Pearse   Cross-city buses

O'SULLIVAN ANTIQUES

A seasoned expert on the Irish antiques scene, Chantal O'Sullivan's has a keen eye for exquisite items from years gone by. You'll find everything from mahogany furniture to marble mantelpieces, garden statues and delicate glass.

J9   43–4 Francis Street   454 1143   68A, 78A, 123

SILVER SHOP

Wide range of antique silver and silver-plate from the conventional to the unusual. Prices start low and head up into the thousands. Great for imaginative gifts.

K9   1st Floor, Powerscourt Townhouse Centre, Clarendon Street   679 4147
Pearse   Cross-city buses

TEMPLE BAR

CHRISTOPHER
A small shop stacked with clubbing clothing for the street wise.

✉ 12 Crown Alley
☎ 679 8891

CUAN HANLY
Cuan Hanly is Ireland's most fashionable bespoke men's tailor. His flagship emporium also stocks his off-the-peg label plus other men and women's clothing, accessories, furniture and magazines.

✉ 1 Pudding Row
☎ 671 1406

DESIGNYARD
A centre for crafts and decorative arts. (The first floor is home to the Irish Crafts Council gallery, ► 76.) Note how the floor mosaic traces the path of an underground river, and the wrought iron gates imitate a Dublin street map. The jewellery gallery downstairs showcases Irish designers.

✉ 12 East Essex Street
☎ 677 8453

FORBIDDEN PLANET
This shop is packed to the rafters with comics, rare photos, postcards and pop-culture memorabilia. Of equal appeal to children and those old enough to know better!

✉ 5–6 Crampton Quay
☎ 671 0688

GALLERY OF PHOTOGRAPHY
Two small but well-designed floors of exhibition space. A ground-floor shop sells postcards, posters, images and a good range of specialist photography books.

✉ Meeting House Square
☎ 671 4654

GREEN BUILDING
Haus is one of Dublin's leading contemporary homeware stores. Owned by furniture enthusiast Garett O'Hagan, this is where Dublin style gurus pick up designer items and accessories. The premises are entirely eco-friendly, with solar and wind-generated electricity, waste recycling and other green features.

✉ Haus, 3–4 Crow Street
☎ 679 5155

ROMAN SMITH
The fashion pack's favourite place for stylish shoes imported in small batches from abroad. Good, diverse labels plus lots of locally-sourced accessories. Colourful, feminine and fun.

✉ 6 Sprangers Yard, Crow Street
☎ 670 3161

SKATE CITY
Clive Rowan's upstairs shop is full of skate gear from the US, as well as his own fleeces, shirts and baggies. Also stocks skate, surf and snow-boards plus accessories.

✉ Crown Alley   ☎ 679 9900

THE SOURCE
The popularity of this extraordinary interiors shop is as wide reaching as its stock. Everything is bright, colourful, functional and totally whacky. Sells unique stock at accessible prices.

✉ Temple Bar   ☎ 677 2255

Temple Bar takes off

In the late 1980s, there were plans afoot to build a new bus terminus in Temple Bar, named for Sir William Temple, who bought the land during the 16th century. Fortunately Dubliners' vociferous objections prevailed, and the city's 'left bank' began to take off. Today the area is pedestrian-friendly, and vehicle access is restricted. And there's always something happening: an outdoor film screening or music recital, or special events like the Blues Festival, Jazz Festival and the Taste of Temple Bar Food Festival.

For up-to-date news of what's on, drop into the information centre at 18 Eustace Street ☎ 671 5717.

➕ K9 ✉ Between Dame Street and the south quays

🚇 Tara Street

🚌 Cross-city buses

IRISH CRAFTS

Made in Ireland

If you're looking for something of modern Ireland that will enhance your home, check out the following shops favoured by Irish people as well as visitors:

Jerpoint glass jugs, glasses, bowls and candlesticks are heavy, hand-blown pieces of simple design with occasional colour bursts.

Irish fashion designer John Rocha has brought Waterford crystal up to date and back into fashion with a designer line that is minimalist and popular with younger buyers. His glasses, bowls, vases and platters come in three styles.

Nicholas Mosse's sponged pottery is so popular that Tiffany & Co has commissioned a pattern. His colourful table settings, jugs, bowls and kitchenware are a delight.

Simon Pearse's approach to ceramics is zen-like. Lines are pure and uncluttered and the shapes of the stoneware are natural and organic. Unadorned, and often unglazed, the durable pieces are sturdy and beautiful.

AVOCA

Irish fashions, speciality foods, books, jewellery and gifts in this up-market shop that has branches across Ireland. The selection of merchandise combines the traditional with the fashionable and known brands with own label. Above all, the stock is high quality, bright and original.

➕ K9 ✉ 11 Suffolk Street ☎ 677 4215 🚆 Pearse 🚌 Cross-city buses

CELTIC NOTE

One of the country's best specialist Irish music shops has everything from classical to traditional, rock to contemporary.

✉ K9 ✉ Nassau Street ☎ 670 4157 🚆 Pearse 🚌 Cross-city buses

CRAFTS CENTRE OF IRELAND

Good selection of Irish crafts not readily available in other shops – whimsical rugs, watercolours, mirrors, candlesticks, a variety of pottery, glass and ironwork.

➕ K9 ✉ Top Floor, Street Stephen's Green Centre ☎ 475 4526 🚆 Pearse 🚌 Cross-city buses

HOUSE OF IRELAND

Traditional Irish fashion, crafts, crystal, china and Aran knitwear. A good source for coats of arms.

➕ K9 ✉ 38 Nassau Street ☎ 671 6133 🚆 Pearse 🚌 Cross-city buses

IRISH CRAFTS COUNCIL

Elegant pieces by Ireland's leading craftspeople. You can also commission special pieces.

➕ K9 ✉ Design Yard, East Essex Street ☎ 677 8453 🚆 Tara Street 🚌 Cross-city buses

KILKENNY

Dublin's finest showcase for Celtic crafts. An essential stopping point for stylish Irish decorative objects for the home, glass, books, fashion and jewellery.

➕ K9 ✉ Nassau Street ☎ 677 7066 🚆 Pearse 🚌 Cross-city buses

LOUIS MULCAHY

Louis Mulcahy is one of Ireland's most prolific ceramicists, and this spacious shop is a perfect showcase for his extensive range of pottery items. Packaging and shipping is easily arranged by helpful staff.

➕ K9 ✉ 46 Dawson Street ☎ 670 9311 🚆 Pearse 🚌 Cross-city buses

TOWER CENTRE

Inspiring potters, wood turners, jewellers and textile designers work and sell in around 35 small workshops here. Look for pieces by quirky silversmith Alan Ardiff, scarves by Mel Bradly (who also works for John Rocha and Louise Kennedy) and pottery by Mark English, whose tableware is used at the Viking Adventure banquets (▶ 32, 58). Just a short walk from Trinity College.

✉ L9 ✉ Pearse Street ☎ 677 5655 🚆 Pearse 🚌 13

FOOD & WINE

BIG CHEESE COMPANY

In addition to a huge variety of cheeses from varied sources worldwide, this shop also stocks imported foods from America, France, Italy and Belgium. It's the only place in Dublin for delicacies like Neuhaus chocolate, Maxim's de Paris coffee and suggestively shaped pasta.

K9 · 14/15 Trinity Street
671 1399 · Pearse
Cross-city buses

DOUGLAS FOOD COMPANY

Epicurean haven for those in a hurry, with the best caviar, *foie gras*, pastries and French cheese.

M12 · 53 Main Street, Donnybrook · 269 4066
10, 46a

THE EPICUREAN FOOD HALL

Home-made ice cream, sweet pastries, bagels, vegetarian and organic sellers contend with each other for the most divine smells each day.

K8 · Upper Liffey Street
Tara Street · Cross-city buses

HOUSE OF LIME AND LEMONGRASS

Additive-free pasta sauces, chutneys, mustards, bottled olives, roast garlic and sun-dried tomatoes.

K8 · 2–3 Mary's Abbey, Capel Street · 872 2965
Cross-city buses

LE MAISON DES GOURMANDS

A mouth-watering array of patisserie sit in the window of this eponymous food hall; inside are savoury treats and the finest French packaged goods.

K9 · 115 Castle Market
672 7258 · Pearse
Cross-city buses

MAGILLS

Salami, meats, bread, cheese, coffee and every sort of packaged delicacy you can imagine.

K9 · 14 Clarendon Street
671 3830 · Pearse
Cross-city buses

MITCHELL & SON WINE MERCHANTS

The ground floor houses Dublin's oldest and possibly finest wine merchants stocking interesting and exclusive vintages. Crowds gather for lunch and dinner in the popular Bruno's restaurant (► 63).

L9 · 21 Kildare Street
676 0766 · Pearse
Cross-city buses

THE OLIVE MAN

Over 25 different sorts of olives, plus sun-dried and spiced vegetables. Divinely scented hand-made soaps.

K9 · George's Street Arcade, South Great Georges Street · Cross-city buses

SHERIDANS CHEESE SHOP

This glorious shop packed with massive blocks of cheese is a wonderful showcase for the Irish farmhouse varieties that are winning awards worldwide.

K9 · South Anne's Street
679 3143 · Pearse
Cross-city buses

Saturday market

Irish food lovers spend their Saturday mornings in Meeting House Square at Temple Bar, where the weekly market sells organic produce, exotic meats, delicious pre-cooked meals, pastries and farmhouse cheeses. It poses just one dilemma – can you resist tucking into your purchases before the next meal?

THEATRE

Festival

You would expect the capital of literary Ireland to be overflowing with theatrical talent – and you would be right. *Riverdance* and *Dancing at Lughnasa* both played to Irish audiences before receiving global acclaim, and Martin McDonagh packed Dubliners in to see his *Lenane* trilogy prior to winning several Tony awards on Broadway. In contrast, the annual Christmas pantomimes see Irish celebrities ham up traditional fairytales, usually with elaborate story embellishment and even more extravagant costumes. The Dublin Theatre Festival and fringe continues to grow in breadth, stature and popularity each year. Events are staged throughout September in traditional and less conventional locations around the city and tickets are usually available at short notice.

ABBEY

The national theatre played a vital role in the renaissance of Irish culture at the end of the 19th century and the quality of the Abbey's playwriting and performances is rarely surpassed. Many first runs go on to London's West End or New York's Broadway.

✚ L8 ✉ 26 Lower Abbey Street ☎ 878 7222 🚇 Connelly/Tara Street 🚌 Cross-city buses

ANDREW'S LANE

The main stage and a smaller studio upstairs attract a steady stream of young theatregoers.

✚ K9 ✉ Andrew's Lane ☎ 679 5720 🚇 Pearse 🚌 Cross-city buses

FOCUS THEATRE

This tiny space has seen many surprises and excellent performances. Movie superstar Gabriel Byrne was once a regular.

✚ L10 ✉ 6 Pembroke Place, off Pembroke Street ☎ 676 3071 🚌 10

GAIETY

An integral part of Dublin theatreland, with a varied programme of pantomime, opera, musicals, comedies, classic plays and touring shows. After the curtain goes down, from Thursday to Saturday, the theatre's bars become groovy jazz and samba nightclubs.

✚ K9 ✉ South King Street ☎ 677 1717 🚇 Pearse 🚌 Cross-city buses

GATE

Some of Dublin's most inspired and sophisticated theatre, performed in an 18th-century building. Many Dublin thespians and critics rate the works performed here as the best in Ireland. Showcases new Irish playwrights.

✚ K8 ✉ Cavendish Row ☎ 874 4045 🚌 Cross-city buses

OLYMPIA

Dublin's oldest theatre mounts mainstream shows including musicals, stand-up comedy and pantomimes that continue well beyond Christmas. Late at night, the venue (▶ 81) reverberates to the sound of live bands from Ireland and abroad. Rumour has it that the backstage ghost is alive and well.

✚ K9 ✉ 74 Dame Street ☎ 677 7744 🚌 Cross-city buses

PEACOCK

The Abbey's younger sibling, part of the same complex, is a platform for the work of emerging Irish talent.

✚ L8 ✉ 26 Lower Abbey Street ☎ 878 7222 🚇 Connelly/Tara Street 🚌 Cross-city buses

PROJECT ARTS CENTRE

Young theatre groups stage new and experimental performances at lunchtime, in the evening and late at night.

✚ K9 ✉ East Essex Street, ☎ 1850 260027 🚇 Tara Street 🚌 Cross-city buses

CINEMA

AMBASSADOR CINEMA

This two-screen cinema was once an elaborate theatre. The upholstery is faded but romantic couples appreciate the double seats. Most Dubliners have seen a Disney classic here as children.

✚ K8 ✉ Parnell Square ☎ 872 7000 🚌 Cross-city buses

CLASSIC

Old-fashioned cinema with weekly Friday-night interactive screening of the Rocky Horror Show.

✚ H13 ✉ Harolds Cross ☎ 492 3699 🚌 54A

IRISH FILM CENTRE

Members and guests can view arthouse or limited release films on the two screens in this interesting conversion of old houses. Restaurant, bar, shop and film archive. Membership (reasonably priced) can be arranged on the spot.

✚ K9 ✉ 6 Eustace Street, Temple Bar ☎ 679 3477 🚊 Tara Street 🚌 Cross-city buses

ORMONDE

The only cinema worth visting on Dublin's south side. Five screens show a mixture of new releases and children's films.

✚ N16 ✉ Lower Kilmacud Road, Stillorgan ☎ 278 0000 🚌 46A

PARNELL CENTRE

The centre houses a nine-screen UCG multiplex, together with a range of entertainment including simulated rides, computer games, well-supervised amusements, themed bar and restaurants, fast food outlets, virtual reality experiences and a car park. Shooters bar is a very popular spot with young people with its sports theme and very loud music. You could spend hours here without catching a glimpse of daylight.

✚ K8 ✉ Parnell Street ☎ 872 8444/872 8400 🚌 Cross-city buses

SAVOY

This old-style cinema hosts most Irish film premieres and their parties. Modern concessions include five wide screens, drink holder and Dolby sound systems.

✚ K8 ✉ O'Connell Street ☎ 874 6000 🚌 Cross-city buses

SCREEN

Fringe and mainstream films on three screens. Good discounts on matinees. Bring your own munchies – the selection here leaves much to be desired.

✚ K8 ✉ D'Olier Street ☎ 672 5500 🚊 Pearse 🚌 Cross-city buses

STER CENTURY

Ireland's biggest and newest multiplex has 12 screens including The Big Fella, Europe's largest. Seats look and feel like sports cars, sound and picture quality are state of the art, as are the snacks and café facilities.

✚ Off map to northwest ✉ Liffey Valley Centre ☎ 605 5700 🚌 78A

Did you know?

• James Joyce was a manager at one of Ireland's earliest cinemas, the Volta, which opened in 1909.

• Dublin has one of the highest per capita cinema attendances in Europe.

• The Irish Film Centre, the Savoy and the Screen are all venues for the Dublin film festival in March.

• Seats are cheaper during the day.

• There is a no-smoking policy in all cinemas.

CLASSICAL & OPERA

Classical Irish – the next generation

The Irish are never slow to come forward with a song, and while one tier of artists such as Boyzone and The Corrs are topping the pop music charts, there is another group of performers who are making similar waves in the classical world.

Riverdance changed global views of traditional Irish music, infusing familiar rhythms and dance steps with inspirational melodies and choreography. An essential ingredient to this phenomenon was the a capella vocals of Aunua – a 40-strong choral group who can often be seen performing Gregorian, classical and original pieces to enthusiastic audiences. Equally captivating are the delicate but powerful Vard sisters. These two thirtysomething Dubliners have already topped the charts with their recordings, whilst always rewarding live audiences with pitch-perfect performances of classical favourites.

Look out for CDs from these performers as well as the Irish Tenors who are currently touring the world with sell-out shows of popular Irish ballads and songs.

Dublin has a thriving classical music and opera scene, though an irregular frequency of performances. The National Concert Hall stages a full programme but other venues offer seasonal performances only. To find out about forthcoming events, call the box offices direct or check the listings in the *Irish Times*. Booking is recommended for most performances.

BANK OF IRELAND ARTS CENTRE

Classical recitals by amateur and professional groups from Ireland and overseas.

➕ K9 ✉ Foster Place
☎ 671 1488

HUGH LANE MUNICIPAL GALLERY OF MODERN ART

Classical recitals are held at noon every Sunday in this impressive art gallery. Admission is free and the programme runs year-round with a break in summer.

➕ K7 ✉ Parnell Square North
☎ 874 1903 🚇 Connolly
🚌 Cross-city buses

MUSIC IN GREAT IRISH HOUSES

A summer programme of classical recitals in grand Irish houses, many of them in or around Dublin.

☎ 278 1528

NATIONAL CONCERT HALL

Busy Georgian concert hall with a modern auditorium and superb world-class acoustics. Top artists perform here when they are in town. The John Field Room, the National Concert Hall's annex space hosts performances of chamber music among its varied programme of modern and classical music. It has a seating capacity of 250.

➕ K10 ✉ Earlsfort Terrace
☎ 475 1572

OPERA IRELAND

The Gaiety Theatre (► 78) plays host to Dublin's most professional and prolific opera society. The twice-yearly programmes (usually held before Easter and Christmas) include much-loved favourites as well as more obscure works.

☎ 453 5519

THE PROMS

This annual week-long mid-May season takes place at a different venue each year. Coordinated and recorded for broadcast by Ireland's national television station.

➕ Venue varies ☎ 208 2977 or 208 2773

ROYAL DUBLIN SOCIETY

The regular series of lunchtime and evening recitals in the RDS library has attracted a faithful following of music buffs, society ladies and RDS members.

➕ N11 ✉ Merrion Road
☎ 668 0645 🚇 Lansdowne Road 🚌 5, 7, 7A, 7X, 8, 45, 84

BARS & LIVE MUSIC

BAGGOT INN
Traditional music is alive and well in this long-established pub, now owned by Jack Charlton, the national football team's former manager.

✚ L10 ✉ Lower Baggot Street ☎ 676 1430 🚊 Pearse 🚌 10

JOHNNY FOXES
People come from near and far for the turf fires, live traditional music, céilí dancing and delicious seafood. If you want to eat, be sure to book ahead.

✚ Off map to southwest ✉ Dublin Mountains, Glencullen, County Dublin ☎ 295 5647 🚌 44B

HOGAN'S
A fashionable bar packed with Dublin's beautiful young things on their way to nearby dance clubs.

✚ K9 ✉ 35 South Great Georges Street ☎ 677 5904 🚌 Cross-city buses

HQ
A superb city centre venue with a hugely varied roster of performing acts. There's an emphasis on service, with good bars, a casual restaurant and plenting of seating to be had. Also at the same address is the Hall of Fame, tracing Irish music from early times to the present day.

✚ K8 ✉ Middle Abbey Street ☎ 878 3345 🚊 Tara Street 🚌 Cross-city buses

THE LONG HALL
Time seems to have stood still in this traditional hostelry, with a long bar, smoked glass and beautiful paintwork.

✚ K9 ✉ 51 South Great Georges Street ☎ 475 1590 🚌 Cross-city buses

MIDNIGHT AT THE OLYMPIA
Midnight concerts in Dublin's oldest theatre are massively popular on the live circuit.

✚ K9 ✉ 74 Dame Street ☎ 677 7744 🚌 Cross-city buses

STAG'S HEAD
Built in 1770 and remodelled in 1895, this pub has kept its wonderful stained-glass windows, wood carvings and iron work. Off a cobblestoned lane – follow the brass sign in the Dame Street sidewalk.

✚ K9 ✉ 1 Dame Court ☎ 679 3701 🚌 Cross-city buses

TEMPLE BAR MUSIC CENTRE
A premier music venue that also stages fashion shows, club nights and dance events. Café, bar and good live music. Upstairs balcony.

✚ K9 ✉ Curved Street ☎ 670 9202 🚊 Tara Street 🚌 Cross-city buses

WHELAN'S
A well-run venue with good acoustics, plenty of space and a great atmosphere. Up-and-coming Irish groups and overseas bands on tour are often headline.

✚ K10 ✉ 25 Wexford Street ☎ 478 0766 🚌 14, 14A, 47, 47A, 47B, 83

Craic
Craic (pronounced 'crack') describes fun, laughter, chat and an overall good time. In Ireland, people, places and events can all be 'great craic'.

Cheers!
When toasting each other, Irish people say 'sláinte!' (pronounced slawn-cha) meaning 'health!' It certainly gets easier to say as the night progresses.

Comic relief
If you fancy a pint with plenty of attitude but no music, head for Murphy's Laughter Lounge, Dublin's first dedicated comedy club. It has the added bonus of a lively bar open late.

✚ K8 ✉ 4–6 Eden Quay ☎ 1800 266339 🚊 Tara Street 🚌 Cross-city buses

CLUBS

Dance

When looking for the best dance clubs in Dublin, go by the name of that particular night at the club rather than the name of the venue itself. Most good dance nights are independently run gigs organised by promotors and staged in different places around town. *The Event Guide*, distributed free in bars and cafés around the city, has the most comprehensive and accurate listings. Top Dublin promoters and nights to look out for include Influx (techno/house), Strictly Handbag (1980s and retro) and 3345 – a day to night extravaganza held at Vicar Street on the last Sunday of each month.

Gay scene

HAM at The PoD every Friday is Dublin's most happening gay clubnight. For pre-club drinks and dance nights try The George on South Great Georges Street (Sunday Bingo is especially popular). Don't miss the Alternative Miss Ireland (an outrageous drag beauty pageant) if you are in town on St Patrick's Festival – around 17 March.

CLUB ANNABEL'S

One of Dublin's largest and most successful clubs. Frequented by young professionals who like to party.

✚ L11 ✉ Burlington Hotel, Upper Leeson Street ☎ 660 5222 🚌 13, 46A

THE KITCHEN

Ultra-hip dance club in the basement of U2's cosmopolitan Clarence Hotel. The style of the music and clubbers varies dramatically from night to night, so check the local press for details of what's on.

✚ K9 ✉ Clarence Hotel, 6–8 Wellington Quay ☎ 677 6635 🚆 Tara Street 🚌 Cross-city buses

LILLIE'S BORDELLO

This recently refurbished, well-established club is a home-away-from-home for international pop and film stars. House, chart and oldie music.

✚ K9 ✉ Adam Court, Grafton Street ☎ 679 9204 🚆 Pearse 🚌 Cross-city buses

THE PALACE

Dublin's first super-club that fits hoards of happy young dancers. Music is a mainstream mish-mash of popular dance tunes.

✚ K910 ✉ Camden Street ☎ 478 0808 🚆 Pearse 🚌 Cross-city buses

POD

The Place of Dance is still the hippest club in town, and the tight door policy restricts entry to the stylish and sober. There's a different club each evening but you'll find a good mix of happy house and dance floor favourites. Chocolate Bar and The Red Box are adjacent.

✚ K10 ✉ 35 Harcourt Street ☎ 478 0166 🚌 Cross-city buses

RENARDS

Late-night club with busy basement dance floor, a ground-floor café/bar and an upstairs VIP area populated by thirtysomethings from the worlds of fashion, media and film. In this club music comes second to the frantic chat.

✚ L9 ✉ 33–5 South Frederick Street ☎ 677 5874 🚆 Pearse 🚌 Cross-city buses

RÍRÁ

A favourite of students, no-nonsense clubbers and other Dubliners looking for a good night out. Informal and fashionable with a chill-out area upstairs.

✚ K9 ✉ 1 Exchequer Street ☎ 677 4835 🚆 Tara Street 🚌 Cross-city buses

TEMPLE THEATRE

Roomy venue that does other one-off dance nights, about 2km from the city centre on the wrong side of town – but getting there is worth the effort (do exercise caution when you leave and order a taxi to get home).

✚ K7 ✉ Temple Street ☎ 874 5425 🚌 11, 11A, 11B, 16, 16A, 36, 36A, 36B

SPORTS

FOOTBALL

Since the World Cup in 1990, the Irish have become football fanatics, and Dublin usually stands still when the national team plays. The season runs from August to May, and you can buy tickets for matches at Tolka Park Stadium (shared home to Shamrock Rovers and Shelbourne Rovers), at the stiles.

🞤 K4 ✉ Tolka Park Stadium, Griffith Avenue ☎ 837 9602

GAELIC GAMES

Gaelic football and hurling are fast, physical games and the All-Ireland finals are played before sell-out crowds in early and late September. Hurling is an ancient sport whose roots go back to pre-Christian times, and both games have been actively promoted by the Gaelic Athletic Association since 1884.

🞤 L6/7 ✉ Croke Park Stadium ☎ 836 3222 🚌 3, 11, 16, 123

GOLF

The growth of championship golf courses in Dublin is staggering. Many clubs welcome non-members and fees are reasonable. The most famous are Royal Dublin and Portmarnock; also try Castle, Grange, Woodbrook Malahide, Miltown, Hermitage and Island. Or try one of the city's pitch-and-putt courses. The Irish Open Golf Championships are staged in July and rotate around different courses in the country.

GREYHOUND RACING

Catch this popular activity on Wednesday, Thursday and Saturday.

🞤 N10 ✉ Shelbourne Park Stadium, South Lotts Road ☎ 668 3502 🚌 Lansdowne Road 🚌 3

HORSE RACING

Leopardstown Race Course is one of Ireland's busiest. Open all year, it hosts the Hennessy Gold Cup and traditional post-Christmas festival, among other events.

🞤 Off map to south ✉ Leopardstown Road ☎ 289 3607 🚌 86, 114

ROLLERBLADING

The smooth, flat, picturesque walk along Sandymount Strand is popular with local in-line skaters who whoosh up and down the seafront day and night. A stunning location in spring and summer.

🞤 O11 ✉ Sandymount Strand, Sandymount 🚌 1, 3, 7A, 7X, 8, 45, 8

RUGBY

Ireland's fans remain enthusiastic despite the national team's changing fortunes. Details of fixtures at local clubs, like Bective Rangers, Wesley and Blackrock, are published in the local press. Better, soak up the atmosphere of a major tournament at Lansdowne Road or in one of the many pubs showing the match on screen.

🞤 N10 ✉ Lansdowne Road Stadium, Ballsbridge ☎ 668 4601 🚌 Lansdowne Road 🚌 6, 7, 7A, 7X, 8, 45, 84

The Irish game

The Gaelic Athletic Association (GAA) is Ireland's largest sporting and cultural organisation. Their newly-opened museum dedicated to the national games, is housed in the home of Gaelic sport, Croke Park, and well worth a visit. Interactive, and with plenty to educate and enthuse visitors, the exhibition gives the past, present and future of popular Irish sport.

GAA Museum

🞤 L7 ✉ New Stand, Croke Park, Jones Road ☎ 855 8176 🚌 3, 11, 11A, 16, 16A, 123

Snooker

Jason's Snooker Hall is home to Ken Doherty and a host of rising stars.

🞤 K11 ✉ 56 Ranelagh ☎ 497 5983 🚌 11, 11A, 11B, 13, 18, 44, 44B, 48, 62

LUXURY HOTELS

Prices

For a double room per night:

Luxury   IR$150 and above

Mid-Range   1R$60–IR£150

Budget   under IR$60

Dublin hotel rates historically included bed, full Irish breakfast, service charge and VAT (currently 21 per cent) in the quoted price, but with the arrival of so many new international chains to the capital, it is always wise to check when booking.

Special deals

Many hotels and guest houses offer special weekend packages of bed, breakfast and evening meals at greatly reduced rates. Telephone ahead to see what's available or check the back page of the *Irish Times*. High season runs from Easter to October; bargains are most numerous at other times of year.

BERKELEY COURT

Superlative comfort and tranquility with chintz sofas, thick carpets and blissful quiet.

🏠 N11 🖂 Lansdowne Road ☎ 660 1711, fax 661 7238 🚇 Lansdowne Road 🚌 5, 7, 7A, 7X, 8, 45, 46 84

CLARENCE

Chic, modern interior with soft suede upholstery and stunning floral arrangements. Bedrooms are small, apart from the fine duplex penthouse.

🏠 K9 🖂 6–8 Wellington Quay ☎ 670 9000, fax 670 7800 🚇 Tara Street 🚌 Cross-city buses

CLARION STEPHEN'S HALL

Tastefully furnished all-suite hotel. Rooms have state-of-the-art office facilities. Fine restaurant.

🏠 L10 🖂 14–7 Lower Leeson Street ☎ 638 1111, fax 638 1122 🚌 10, 46A, cross-city buses

FITZWILLIAM

Stylishly designed by Terence Conran, with a superb restaurant.

🏠 K9 🖂 St Stephen's Green ☎ 662 5155, fax 676 7488 🚌 Cross-city buses

HERBERT PARK

Modern, bright, airy hotel in Dublin's exclusive residential area. Quiet comfort with rooms overlooking Herbert Park.

🏠 N10 🖂 Ballsbridge ☎ 667 2200, fax 667 2595 🚇 Lansdowne Road 🚌 5, 7, 7A, 7X, 8, 45, 46 84

JURYS TOWERS

Large, well-appointed rooms with excellent facilities and a secluded library and lounge.

🏠 N10 🖂 Lansdowne Road ☎ 667 0033, fax 660 6640 🚇 Lansdowne Road 🚌 5, 7, 7A, 7X, 8, 45, 46 84

MERRION

This impressive hotel, originally four Georgian houses, has luxurious bedrooms with good business facilities and spacious bathrooms, and an 18th-century garden. Gym, pool and spa.

🏠 L10 🖂 Upper Merrion Street ☎ 603 0600, fax 603 0700 🚇 Pearse 🚌 5, 7, 7A, 7X, 8, 10, 18, 45, 46

THE MORRISON

Modern designer heaven, every inch of the Morrison is east-meets-west cosmopolitan. Vibrant, young guests converge on the lobby, bars and restaurants at all times.

🏠 M10 🖂 Eastmoreland Place ☎ 668 7666, fax 660 2655 🚌 10, 18

THE SHELBOURNE

This historic hotel is an integral part of Dublin society, with friendly service, a gentle charm and rooms overlooking the green.

🏠 L9 🖂 27 St Stephen's Green ☎ 676 6471, fax 661 6006 🚌 Cross-city buses

WESTBURY

In the heart of Dublin's shopping district. You can watch Dublin life come and go from the wonderful open foyer.

🏠 K9 🖂 Grafton Street ☎ 679 1122, fax 679 7078 🚇 Pearse 🚌 Cross-city buses

MID-RANGE HOTELS

88

The excellent service in this Georgian-style house has won it a loyal following. Executive boardroom and access to local health club.

➕ M10 ✉ 88 Pembroke Road ☎ 660 0277, fax 660 0291 🚇 Lansdowne Road 🚌 5, 7, 7A, 7X, 8, 10, 18, 45, 46 84

HARRINGTON HALL

A beautifully restored Georgian guesthouse with genteel public areas and generously proportioned bedrooms. An elegant address in the city centre.

➕ K10 ✉ 70 Harcourt Street ☎ 475 3497, fax 475 4544 🚌 Cross-city buses

JURYS INN

Rates are calculated on a per room basis (up to three adults, or two adults with two children). Lovely bar and restaurant plus car parking facilities.

➕ J9; L8 ✉ Christchurch Place; Custom House Quay ☎ 607 0000, fax 660 9625 🚌 Cross-city buses; 25, 25A, 26,

MESPIL

Efficient, spacious and modern; near the Grand Canal and convenient for business travellers.

➕ L10 ✉ Mespil Road ☎ 667 1222, fax 667 1244 🚌 10, 11, 11A, 11B, 13, 46A, 46B

MOLESWORTH COURT

These pleasantly decorated one- and two-bedroom apartments can be rented for one night or more. Homely, quiet and near Grafton Street.

➕ L9 ✉ Schoolhouse Lane, off Molesworth Street ☎ 676 4799, fax 676 4982 🚇 Pearse 🚌 Cross-city buses

THE MORGAN

This gem of a hotel has Egyptian cotton sheets, spacious bathrooms and excellent in-room facilities including ISDN lines, VCRs and compact disc players. Excellent accommodation at a reasonable price.

➕ K9 ✉ 10 Fleet Street, Temple Bar ☎ 679 3939, fax 679 3946 🚇 Tara Street 🚌 Cross-city buses

PORTMARNOCK HOTEL & GOLF LINKS

Comfort, good food and world-class golf. The hotel's 18-hole course was designed by Bernhard Langer. Near the airport.

➕ Off map to northeast ✉ Strand Road, Portmarnock ☎ 846 0611, fax 846 2442 🚇 Portmarnock 🚌 32, 32A, 32X, 102, 230

STAUNTON'S ON THE GREEN

Large Georgian guest house with garden and well-equipped rooms within easy reach of museums, shops and galleries.

➕ K10 ✉ 83 St Stephen's Green ☎ 478 2300, fax 478 2263 🚌 11, 11A, 11B, 13, 19, 19A, 22, 22A, 46A, 46B

TRINITY LODGE

Elegant Georgian accommodation opposite Trinity College. Large, beautifully decorated rooms.

➕ L9 ✉ 12 South Frederick Street ☎ 679 5044, fax 679 5223 🚇 Pearse 🚌 Cross-city buses

Room in the City

The number of hotel rooms in Dublin has risen dramatically since the mid-1990s. Even with all this extra availability and with the increased popularity of Dublin as a holiday and a business destination, it is always advisable to secure hotel accommodation before arriving in the city.

BUDGET ACCOMMODATION

Budget stay

Budget accommodation comes in three different formats.

Hotels: Dublin city centre is well supplied with clean, functional new hotels that offer somewhere to stay at the right price. Most of the smarter bets are situated around the Temple Bar area and are popular with visiting groups.

Hostels: Forget the traditional image, Dublin has a good selection of very low cost hostels that give guests the option of single or double bedrooms as well as the more usual dorms. Many offer good cafés, laundry rooms and internet access.

Guest houses: There are many reputable bed-and-breakfast establishments working within the auspices of the Irish Tourist Board. Information from the Dublin Tourist Authority ☎ 605 7777

Trinity College

If you are planning a long stay in the summer, it is possible to rent student rooms in Trinity College (☎ 608 2358) at reasonable rates. Some have their own bathrooms and kitchens.

ASTON HOUSE
A tranquil hotel situated in the middle of Temple Bar, the Aston manages to convey a feeling of calm while all outside is hectic. Popular with groups.
➕ K9 ✉ 7–9 Aston Quay ☎ 677 9300, fax 677 9007 🚌 Cross-city buses

AVALON HOUSE
This purpose-built hostel offers single, double and dormitory rooms, in neat, fresh surroundings. Facilities include a casual café and use of internet.
➕ K9 ✉ 55 Aungier Street ☎ 475 0001, fax 475 0303 🚌 Cross-city buses

BARNACLES TEMPLE BAR HOUSE
A more upmarket hostel with communal TV room, self catering facilities and breakfast room. All rooms come with own shower. Location is perfect for those into the buzz of Temple Bar.
➕ K9 ✉ 1 Cecilia Street ☎ 671 6277, fax 671 6591 🚌 Cross-city buses

BEWLEY'S NEWLANDS CROSS
New hotel with good amenities and spacious bedrooms, furnished to a high standard. The location, slightly outside the city, makes it most suitable if you have a car.
➕ Off map to west ✉ Newland's Cross, Naas Road ☎ 464 0140, fax 464 0900 🚌 51, 51B, 69X

HARDING HOTEL
A superior find in the budget bracket, Hardings looks the part with clever interior design and is packed with atmosphere thanks to a really lively hotel bar.
➕ J9 ✉ Copper Alley, Fishamble Street ☎ 679 6500, fax 679 6504 🚌 Cross-city buses

ISAACS HOSTEL
One of the newer and better Dublin hostels located on the edge of Temple Bar.
➕ K9 ✉ 2–5 Frenchman's Lane ☎ 874 9321, fax 855 6574 🚌 Cross-city buses

KINLAY HOUSE
A good hostel with rooms to suit different budgets – from dormitory-style to en-suite twins. Continental breakfast included.
➕ K9 ✉ 2–12 Lord Edward Street ☎ 679 6644, fax 679 7437 🚌 Cross-city buses

RIVER HOUSE HOTEL
Rather bland, but a good value hotel situated in the middle of Dublin's busy left bank. The hotel bar is very popular.
➕ K9 ✉ 23–24 Eustace Street ☎ 670 7655, fax 670 7650 🚌 Cross-city buses

THE TOWNHOUSE
A remarkable guest house whose opulent and theatrical decor reflects the taste of the building's original owners – 19th-century playwrights Dion Boucicault and Lafcadio Hearn. The location is in a less affluent part of the city centre, so you'll need to take a taxi after dark.
➕ L7 ✉ 47–48 Lower Gardiner Street ☎ 878 8808, fax 878 8787 🚌 41A, 41B, 41C, 41X and cross-city buses

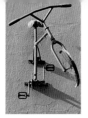

DUBLIN
travel facts

Arriving & Departing

Before you go

- Visitors must have a current passport (or official identity card for EU nationals) valid for the duration of their stay.
- UK citizens do not need a passport but should carry a driver's licence, birth certificate or similar identification.
- The maximum stay permitted in Ireland for non-EU citizens is six months.
- There are no vaccination requirements.
- Car drivers must bring their vehicle registration certificate, insurance certificate (valid for Ireland), driver's licence and display a country sticker.
- Check your insurance coverage before leaving home, and purchase a supplemental policy as necessary.
- EU citizens are covered by reciprocal arrangements for medical expenses. Obtain an E111 form before travelling.

When to go

- Most visitors come between March and October when the weather is at its best and there is a wider choice of activities.
- Some attractions close during the low season.
- You will find the best deals in accommodation from November to February.

Climate

- Dublin weather is unpredictable and you should always be prepared for rain. Layers are the best option, as even in summer sunshine can give way quickly to cooler temperatures.
- Late July to early September is usually the warmest period.

Temperatures can reach as high as 26°C, but drop as low as 12°C.

- Winters are not severe and tend to be wet rather than snowy. Temperatures very rarely fall below freezing.

Arriving by air

- Dublin airport is 12km north of the city. There is only one terminal.
- The *Airlink* express coach service to the city centre operates from 6:40AM to 11PM, with departures every 20–30 minutes. A single fare costs IR£2.50.
- The taxi rank is outside arrivals. Taxis are always metered and a journey to the city centre should cost IR£12–14.
- Several car rental companies are based in the arrivals area.

Arriving by boat

- Ferries from the UK sail into the ports of Dublin and Dun Laoghaire, which is 14km south of the city.
- Taxis and coaches operate from both ports into the city centre. Local buses and the DART light railway are easily accessible from Dun Laoghaire.

Arriving by car

- Traffic drives on the left in Ireland.
- The volume of traffic in Dublin is increasing and parking is expensive and limited.
- Avoid the morning and late afternoon rush hours, keep out of bus lanes and use carparks.
- Traffic wardens take their job seriously and tow-away trucks are plentiful.
- Most hotels and guesthouses have private parking for guests.
- Always lock your car and keep belongings out of sight.
- Men called 'lock 'ards', carrying

rolled up newspapers, may try
to help you find a parking space
at night. If you accept their
unofficial services, a 50p–IR£1 tip
is customary.

Arriving by train

- There are two mainline stations in
  Dublin. Passengers from the
  north of Ireland arrive at Connolly
  Station, while trains from the
  south and west operate in and out
  of Heuston Station. Buses and
  taxis are available at both stations.
- For rail information, call Irish Rail
  ☎ 836 6222

Arriving by bus

- Busáras, the main bus terminus, is
  north of the River Liffey, near the
  quays.

Customs regulations

- There are no restrictions on goods
  brought into Ireland by EU
  citizens for personal use.
- Limits apply for other visitors. If
  in doubt, use the red channel.

Departure/airport tax

- Airport tax for departing
  passengers is usually included in
  the price of your ticket.
- A comprehensive network of
  buses operates from Dublin to
  other parts of Ireland.

ESSENTIAL FACTS

Electricity

- 220V AC. Most hotels have 110V
  shaver outlets. Plugs are three
  square pins.

Etiquette

- Dubliners are very friendly so do
  not be unduly perturbed if
  strangers strike up conversation.
  Trust your instincts.
- Do not expect Dubliners to be

very punctual. Likewise, if you
are invited to someone's home for
dinner, aim to arrive about ten
minutes after the agreed time.
- Groups of friends and acquain-
  tances usually buy drinks in
  rounds and, if you join them, you
  will be expected to participate.

Gay and lesbian travellers

- *Gay Community News*, a free
  monthly newspaper, is available
  from clubs, bars and bookshops.
- Gay and lesbian events in Dublin
  include the Alternative Miss
  Ireland (March), Pride (late June)
  and the Lesbian and Gay Film
  Festival (late July).
- For information and advice,
  contact: Gay Switchboard Dublin
  ☎ 872 1055 🕐 Sun–Fri 8–10PM; Sat 3:30–6PM;
  Lesbian Education and
  Awareness (LEA) ✉ 5 Capel Street
  ☎ 872 0460; Outhouse Gay
  Community and Resource Centre
  ✉ 6 South William Street ☎ 670 6377

Lone and women travellers

- Dublin is relatively safe but you
  need to take sensible precautions.
- After dark, sit downstairs on buses
  or in a busy carriage on trains.
- Take a taxi rather than a late-
  night bus out to the suburbs.
- Keep to well-lit main streets.
  Steer clear of Temple Bar at
  pub/club closing time. Though
  not necessarily dangerous, the
  mobs of people tumbling on to
  the streets can be intimidating.
- Do not stroll around Fitzwilliam
  and Merrion squares, or the
  adjoining streets, late at night.
  They are the city's prime prositi-
  tution areas.

Money matters

- The unit of currency is the Irish
  punt, or pound. IR£1 = 100 pence.
- Notes and coins are issued in

89

similar denominations to sterling. Coins: 1p, 2p, 5p, 10p, 20p, 50p and IR£1. Notes: IR£5, £10, £20, £50, £100.

- On 1 January, 1999, the euro became the official currency of Ireland and the Irish punt became a denomination of the euro. Irish punt notes and coins continue to be legal tender during a transitional period. Euro bank notes and coins are likely to start to be introduced by 1 January, 2002.
- Most shops and businesses accept sterling on a parity exchange rate. This may or may not be to your advantage as currency values fluctuate.
- Banks offer better exchange rates than shops, hotels and bureaux de change.
- The bank at Dublin airport has extended opening hours but charges above average commission.
- Credit cards can be used in most hotels, shops and restaurants and to withdraw cash from automatic teller machines.
- Most large shops, hotels and restaurants will accept travellers' cheques accompanied by some form of identification.

National holidays

- 1 January, 17 March, Good Friday, Easter Monday, first Monday in May, Whit Monday (late May/early June), first Monday in August, All Souls' Day (end October/1 November), 25 and 26 December.
- All pubs and most businesses close on Good Friday. Some shops stay open.

Opening hours

- Museums and sights: open seven days a week, with shorter opening hours on Sunday.
- Shops: six days a week, some seven days. Late-night shopping on Thursday. Supermarkets are open longer hours Wed–Fri.
- Banks: Mon–Fri 10–4; Thu 10–5.

Places of worship

- Although Ireland is predominantly Catholic, most religious groups have places of worship in Dublin.
- Buddhism: Buddhist Centre ✉ 56 Inchicore Road ☎ 453 7427
- Church of Ireland: Christ Church Cathedral ✉ Edward Square ☎ 677 8099; St Patrick's Cathedral ✉ Patrick's Street ☎ 475 4817; St Ann's Church ✉ Dawson Street ☎ 676 7727
- Jewish: Synagogue ✉ 37 Adelaide Road ☎ 676 1734
- Methodist: ✉ 9c Lower Abbey Street ☎ 874 2123
- Mormon: Church of the Latter Day Saints ✉ 48 Bushey Park Road, Terenure ☎ 490 5657
- Muslim: Mosque ✉ 163 South Circular Road ☎ 453 3242
- Roman Catholic: Pro-Cathedral ✉ Marlborough Street ☎ 874 5441; University Church ✉ 87a St Stephen's Green ☎ 478 0616; St Teresa's Church ✉ Clarendon Street, off Grafton Street

Student travellers

- Dublin is very student friendly.
- An International Student Identity Card attracts discounts in many cinemas, theatres, shops, restaurants and attractions.
- Discounts may be available on travel cards for the bus and DART.

Time difference

- Ireland runs on GMT. Clocks go forward one hour from late March to late October.

Tipping

- Tips are not expected in cinemas, petrol stations or in pubs, unless

there is table service.
- IR£1–2 is a customary tip for hair-dressers, porters and doormen.
- (➤ 62 for restaurant tipping.)

Toilets
- Dublin is not renowned for the quality or quantity of its public conveniences. Most people call into a pub or large shop.
- Signs may be in Irish: *mná*: women, *fir*: men.

Tourist information
- ✉ Suffolk Street ☎ 1850 230 330 (within Ireland); 00353 669 792 083 (from outside); website: www.visitdublin.com. Accommodation e-mail: reservations@dublintourism.ie

  Other offices: ✉ Dublin Airport; ✉ Dun Laoghaire Harbour; ✉ Baggot Street Bridge; ✉ The Square, Tallaght Town Centre

Visitors with disabilities
- National Rehabilitation Board (☎ 668 4181) publishes two useful booklets: *Guide for Disabled Persons* and an *Accommodation Guide for Disabled Persons*.
- Disability Federation of Ireland can provide a list of helpful organisations in Dublin ✉ 2 Sandyford Office Park, Dublin 18 ☎ 295 9344
- Irish Wheelchair Association ☎ 853 5366

PUBLIC TRANSPORT

Buses
- Buses are the main form of public transport in Dublin but services can be unreliable. Dublin Bus (Bus Átha Cliath) operates Mon–Sat 6AM–11:30PM, Sun 10AM–11:30PM ☎ 873 4222
- The number and destination (in English and Irish) are displayed on the front. *An Lar* means city centre.
- Tickets can be bought on the bus (exact change needed).

- Timetables and prepaid tickets can be bought from Dublin Bus office or some newsagents (➤ see DART below).
- The Nitelink service operates Thu to Sat to the suburbs. Buses leave on the hour from College Street, D'Olier Street and Westmoreland Street from midnight until 3AM. Tickets cost IR£2.50.

DART
- The DART or Dublin Area Rapid Transit is a light rail service running from Howth in the north to Bray in the south.
- Main city-centre stations are Connolly (north side) and Pearse (south side).
- Trains run every 15 minutes (every 5 minutes during rush hour) Mon–Sat 6:30AM–midnight and less frequently Sun 9:30AM–11PM.
- Irish Rail and Dublin Bus sell a range of combined travel passes – single, family, one-day, four-day, weekly (photograph needed). They are not valid for *Nitelink*, *Airlink*, ferry services or tours.
- All travel passes can be purchased from Dublin Bus ✉ 55 Upper O'Connell Street. Selected newsagents sell some passes.

Taxis
- Taxis are in short supply in Dublin, especially at night.
- Taxi ranks can be found outside hotels, train and bus stations and at locations such as St Stephen's Green, Dame Street, O'Connell Street and Dawson Street.
- Useful numbers: All Fives Taxi ☎ 455 5555; All Sevens Taxi ☎ 677 7777; Metro ☎ 668 3333; National Radio Cabs ☎ 677 2222; VIP Radio Taxis ☎ 478 3333. See local telephone directories for full list.

MEDIA & COMMUNICATIONS

Mailing a letter

- Stamps are sold at post offices, some newsagents, hotels and shops. Books of stamps are available from coin-operated machines outside some post offices.
- Post boxes are green.
- The GPO in O'Connell Street is open Mon–Sat 8–8, Sun 10–6.30. Other post offices are generally open Mon–Fri 9–5:30 and certain city-centre branches open on Saturdays. Some suburban offices close for an hour at lunchtime.

Newspapers and magazines

- Dubliners are media conscious and Irish and UK newspapers are read widely.
- The daily broadsheets, the *Irish Times* and the *Irish Independent*, are printed in Dublin. The *Evening Herald* is on sale Mon–Fri at midday. The major UK tabloids also produce separate Irish editions.
- Ireland produces six Sunday newspapers.
- International magazines and newspapers are sold in: Easons ✉ 40–2 Lower O'Connell Street and Tuthills ✉ Royal Hibernian Way
- For listings check out *In Dublin* and the free *Event Guide*.
- *Hot Press* is Ireland's music magazine, *dSide* is read by fashion-conscious club kids, and *Image* is Ireland's best-selling women's title.

Telephones

- Public telephones use coins or phone cards (sold in IR£2, IR£4 and IR£10 denominations at post offices and newsagents).
- Operator ☎ 10; inland directory enquiries ☎ 1190; cross-channel directory enquiries ☎ 1197; overseas directory enquiries ☎ 1198
- Avoid calling from hotels and guesthouses where charges are high. Look for public phones on streets, in pubs, bars and shopping centres.
- The following may be used in front of local telephone numbers: freefone ☎ 1800; local call rate ☎ 1850; premium rate ☎ 1550

Television and radio

- Radio Telefis Éireann (RTÉ) is the state broadcasting authority.
- RTÉ has three radio stations: Radio 1 (88.5 MHz) for news, arts, chat and easy listening music; 2FM (90.7) is the youth-oriented music station; and FM3 (92 MHz) broadcasts classical music and minority interest programmes.
- RTÉ broadcasts on three television channels – mainstream RTÉ 1, N2 aimed at younger, trendier viewers and the Irish-speaking *Telefis Na Gaeilge* (*TnaG*), which also displays English subtitles.
- TV3 is Ireland's first independent television channel that provides lights entertainment to a young adult audience.
- Satellite, cable and terrestrial channels are available.
- Independent stations: Today FM (100–102 MHz), FM104 and 98FM.

EMERGENCIES

Emergency phone numbers

- Police, fire and ambulance ☎ 999 (free of charge).

Consulates

- Australia ✉ Fitzwilton House, Wilton Place, Dublin 2 ☎ 676 1517
- Belgium ✉ Shrewsbury Road, Dublin 4 ☎ 269 2082

- Canada ✉ St Stephen's Green, Dublin 2
  ☎ 478 1988
- Denmark ✉ 121 St Stephen's Green, Dublin 2 ☎ 475 6404
- Finland ✉ Russell House, Stokes Place, Dublin 2 ☎ 478 1344
- France ✉ 36 Ailesbury Road, Dublin 4 ☎ 260 1666
- Germany ✉ Trimleston Avenue, Booterstown, County Dublin ☎ 269 3011
- Greece ✉ 1 Upper Pembroke Street, Dublin 2 ☎ 676 7254
- Italy ✉ 63 Northumberland Road, Dublin 4 ☎ 660 1744
- Japan ✉ Nutley Building, Merrion Court, Dublin 4 ☎ 269 4244
- Netherlands ✉ 106 Merrion Road, Dublin 4 ☎ 269 3444
- Russia ✉ 184–6 Orwell Road, Dublin 14 ☎ 492 3525
- Spain ✉ 17a Merlyn Park, Sandymount, Dublin 4 ☎ 269 1640
- United Kingdom ✉ 31 Merrion Road, Dublin 4 ☎ 205 3700
- USA ✉ 42 Elgin Road, Ballsbridge, Dublin 4 ☎ 668 8777

Lost property

- Report loss or theft of a passport to the police immediately. Your embassy or consulate can provide further assistance.
- Airport ☎ 704 4633; ferryport ☎ 855 2296 or ☎ 661 0511; train ☎ 836 3333; bus ☎ 703 3055

Medicines and medical treatment

- Ambulance ☎ 999 or 112 (free)
- Hospitals with 24-hour emergency service: St Vincent's ✉ Elm Park, Dublin 4 ☎ 269 4533; Mater ✉ Eccles Street, Dublin 7 ☎ 830 1122
- Daytime dental facilities: Dental Hospital ✉ 20 Lincoln Place ☎ 662 0766. For a list of dentists: Irish Dental Association ✉ Richview, Clonskeagh Road, Dublin 4 ☎ 283 0499
- Minor ailments can usually be treated at pharmacies. However,

only a limited range of medication can be dispensed without a prescription.

- Chemist shops open until 10PM: O'Connell Pharmacy ✉ 55 Lower O'Connell Street, Dublin 1 ☎ 873 0427; Donnybrook Pharmacy ✉ 8 The Mall, Donnybrook, Dublin 4 ☎ 269 5236

Sensible precautions

- Bag snatching is prevalent.
- Keep valuables out of sight.
- Watch handbags and wallets in restaurants, hotels, cafés, shops and cinemas.
- Make a separate note of all passport, ticket, travellers' cheques and credit card numbers.
- Avoid walking in Phoenix Park after dark.

LANGUAGE

Although the Irish language is still alive and studied by all school children, English is the spoken language in Dublin. Spoken Irish is rare but the language is enjoying a revival and is seen as fashionable by a younger set proud of their cultural traditions. You will come across Irish on signposts, buses, trains and official documents and the news (*an nuacht*) is broadcast *as gaeilge* on television and radio. *Telefís Na Gaeilge* is a dedicated Irish language channel with English subtitles.

Some Irish words to look out for:

An Lar	City Centre
Baile Átha Cliath	Dublin
Céilí	Dance
Craic	Fun; laughter; good time
Leitris	Lavatory
Mná:	Ladies
Fir:	Gents
Dia dhuit	Hello
Slán	Goodbye
Sláinte	Cheers

93

INDEX

CityPack
Dublin

Written by   Dr Peter Harbison and Melanie Morris
Edited, designed and produced by
 Publishing

Maps   © Automobile Association Developments Ltd 1999, 2000
City centre maps on inside front and back covers reproduced by
permission of the Director of Ordnance Survey Ireland © Government
of Ireland 2000 (Permit No. 7199).

Fold-out map   Created by Bartholomew Ltd, an imprint of HarperCollins Publishers,
Westerhill Road, Glasgow G64 2QT. www.bartholomewmaps.com
© Bartholomew Ltd 2001. Based on the Ordnance Survey by
permission of the Government of the Republic of Ireland.

Distributed in the United Kingdom by AA Publishing, Norfolk House, Priestley Road,
Basingstoke, Hampshire, RG24 9NY.

The contents of this publication are believed correct at the time of printing. Nevertheless, the
publishers cannot be held responsible for any errors or omissions or for changes in the details
given in this guide or for the consequences of any reliance on the information provided by the
same. Assessments of attractions, hotels, restaurants and so forth are based upon the author's
own personal experience and, therefore, descriptions given in this guide necessarily contain an
element of subjective opinion which may not reflect the publishers' opinion or dictate a
reader's own experiences on another occasion.
We have tried to ensure accuracy in this guide, but things do change and we would be grateful
if readers would advise us of any inaccuracies they may encounter.

A CIP catalogue record for this book is available from the British Library.

ISBN 0 7495 1977 0

Published by AA Publishing (a trading name of Automobile Association Developments
Limited, whose registered office is Norfolk House, Priestley Road, Basingstoke, Hampshire
RG24 9NY. Registered number 1878835).

Colour separation by Daylight Colour Art Pte Ltd, Singapore
Printed and bound by Dai Nippon Printing Co (Hong Kong) Ltd.

Acknowledgements
The Automobile Association wishes to thank the following photographers and libraries for their
assistance in the preparation of this book: Illustrated London News 12; Dublinia, Norton
Associates 28a, 28b; Dublin Tourism 32; Bord Failte 25a, 41a; The Board of Trinity College
Dublin 42b; National Museum of Ireland 25b, 44b; © ADAG, Paris and DACS, London, 46;
Number Twenty Nine Museum 47a, 47b; Duchas, The Heritage Service 48b; Rex Features
Picture Library 60; By kind permission of Guinness Ltd 61b. The remaining photographs are
held in the Association's own library (AA Photo Library) and were taken by Stephen
Whitehorne, with the exception of pages: 5a, 5b, 13b, 17b, 21a, 21b, 22, 29a, 33b, 38a, 38b, 43b,
45a, 45b, 54, 56, 57a, 87a, M Short; 6, 16a, 20, 27a, 33a, 34b, 35a, 35b, 38b, 49a, 50a, 50b, 57b,
Slide File; 23a, W Voysey; 1, 37b, 61a, T King; 6–7, 31a, 34a, 39a, S Day; 49b L Blake.

Cover photographs
Main picture: Michael Diggin. Inset top: AA Photo Library (Wyn Voysey)
Inset bottom: Images Picture Library
UPDATED BY *Melanie Morris* MANAGING EDITOR *Hilary Weston*

Titles in the CityPack series